art of energy

art of energy

20th-century masterpieces in the **eni** art collections

Electa

Cover
Filippo De Pisis
Omaggio a Fattori, detail, 1933

eni.com

Translation
Shanti Evans

Special edition

First edition 2010
Reprint 2015

www.electaweb.com

contents

Roberto Poli

sixty years of artistic curiosity

The story of our art collection is a new story, one that has never been written: the lack of a complete and exhaustive stocktaking of the works in the company's possession and of an in-depth historical analysis of the relations between **eni** and the art world risked eclipsing the accounts and works of artists and intellectuals who were able to make a name for themselves on the Italian and international art scene.

It all started in May 1958, when *Il Giorno*—an innovative newspaper founded at Mattei's behest—promoted a major exhibition at La Permanente in Milan devoted to young Italian artists. Among them were some names that would later become celebrated, such as Piero Dorazio, Roberto Crippa and the brothers Giò and Arnaldo Pomodoro. Enrico Mattei supported the initiative and took a personal interest, revealing what was to become even clearer over the following years, a particular sensibility for and attention to art. All this confirms that culture was, right from the outset, a fundamental element of our identity.

Today, alongside the names of Attilio Bertolucci and the intellectuals of *Il Gatto Selvatico* (Natalia Ginzburg, Leonardo Sciascia, Goffredo Parise, Alberto Moravia) and those of the great movie directors (Bernardo Bertolucci, the Taviani brothers, Gillo Pontecorvo) who collaborated with **eni**, we find those of Giorgio Morandi, Filippo De Pisis, Felice Casorati and Renato Guttuso, the authors of masterpieces that have entered the company's art collection. Far from being considered just a financial investment to be jealously guarded in the corporation's vaults, many of the works by these great artists were at once hung in offices and reception rooms. A "conscious" form of patronage, therefore, to which the contribution of some of the most authoritative critics of those years—like Marco Valsecchi and Roberto Longhi—to the numerous initiatives promoted by **eni** through exhibitions, conferences and international seminars also attests. There are many too who recall Mattei strolling around the galleries of Milan and finding out about the artists whose works he saw there, asking their value, discussing the prices or just gazing in silence at the dreamy landscapes of Filippo De Pisis. So the delight in the work of art shown by Mattei and his successors was something not to be hidden, but promoted, communicated and supported.

The cataloguing of the art collection has been carried out with a very precise aim, that of making public and accessible a previously unknown part of the history of our 20th-century art, taking it around and showing it to people. With this in mind we began in 2008 with Morandi, whose works have traveled to the MoMA in New York, the Hotel des Arts in Toulon and the Museo Morandi in Bologna, and then continued with Casorati, whose paintings were shown at the major exhibition devoted to art deco at Palazzo Roverella in Rovigo in January 2009. These are just the first steps toward the opening up of our extraordinary collection to the general public: we want to continue down this road and the publication of this catalogue is a demonstration of this intent.

According to Ernst Jünger a work of art wastes away and loses its luster in surroundings where it has a price but not a value. At **eni** we have decided to start out from this cultural value, communicating it to an ever broader and more interested public.

the passion for culture
the unpublished history
of **eni**'s art collection

curated by **eni** historical archives

May 10, 1958, was a beautiful sunny morning in Milan, and the air was cool after several days of rain. The city that woke up on that Saturday in May was plastered with symbols and posters inviting people to cast a "vote of responsibility" in the now imminent elections of May 25. Among all the posters the ones that stood out were those of the Christian Democrats, who would establish themselves as the major party, and the Italian Communist Party, which confirmed its role as the main force of opposition.

Milan's attention on that morning in May was also focused on an artistic event, scheduled to be held in the Palazzo della Permanente,[1] at Via Turati 34. A fair number of visitors had already assembled in front of the gates of the building, restored a few years earlier, and was destined to grow over the course of the day. By the end of the evening there were more than a thousand. The reason for so much excitement was the opening of the exhibition "Young Italian Artists" organized by the newspaper *Il Giorno* and promoted by its publisher, the energy man, Enrico Mattei.[2] There were those in Milan who wondered what the founder of **eni**, engaged in those months in negotiations over energy supply in Iran and China, had to do with a group of emerging Italian artists, many of whom were destined to leave their mark on the more recent history of art.[3] There were painters and sculptors of every tendency, from figuration to abstractionism, and of various schools and designations. Prominent among them were the Milanese exponents of the Movimento d'Arte Nucleare (Roberto Crippa, Gianni Dova, Gianni Bertini) and the members of the Roman group Forma (Piero Dorazio, Carla Accardi, Pietro Consagra). There were also the brothers Giò and Arnaldo Pomodoro, on their way to becoming internationally recognized masters of sculpture.

To tell the truth the exhibition at the Permanente should have opened almost a month earlier, on April 19, and ended on May 16. This is what its statute declared, adding that "the exhibition will not award prizes of any kind, in that it intends to remain an informative event." However, some intellectuals, including Marco Valsecchi,[4] author of the preface to the catalogue of the exhibition, saw the exhibition at the Permanente—which would have 130 participants showing a total of 370 paintings and sculptures—as a good opportunity to assess the progress made by young Italian talents and to bring up to date the critical studies, still fixated on the period immediately after the war.

To most people, perhaps, Mattei's patronage of an art exhibition seemed curious at least. And yet the story of that unusual figure, a point of reference in the world of Italian oil, went back many years. It was sometime in the spring of 1952 that Enrico Mattei met Bruno Grossetti, founder of the Galleria dell'Annunciata, one of the most prestigious galleries in Milan, and a friend of artists of the caliber of De Chirico, Morandi, Sironi and De Pisis. Via dell'Annunciata, on which the gallery was located, was adjacent to Mattei's Milanese residence on Via Fatebenefratelli, next to the central police station.

Fiorenzo Tomea
Case di Zoppè (Cadore),
detail, 1949

Grossetti writes: "I often saw him at his desk, set right in front of the window that looked onto those of the gallery's bar ... late in the evening, when he'd finished his work, he used to come down to stretch his legs and drink a coffee. He appeared at the door of the study to talk about art and politics. Sometimes we would go out for a stroll along Via dei Giardini, walking up and down the same street several times."[5]

Mattei's meeting with Grossetti was of fundamental importance, and was also mentioned specifically by Fiorenea Giacobbe, personal secretary of the president of **eni**: "Bruno Grossetti ... told me that, when Mattei came in for a coffee, he went into raptures over his pictures—by Rosai, Campigli, Carrà—asking their price, discussing it, bargaining and sometimes, not infrequently, buying."[6]

Is it possible that those strolls in Milan were at the bottom of Mattei's interest in art? Looking more closely, we realize that the private apartment of the founder of **eni** was at the center of a sort of imaginary quadrilateral, whose vertices were the Pinacoteca di Brera, the Palazzo della Permanente on Via Turati, the Galleria Il Milione near Porta Garibaldi—one of the exhibition spaces most often visited by Mattei along with that of Vittorio Barbaroux—and the Galleria dell'Annunciata.[7] From these galleries came Mattei's earliest purchases, dating from as early as 1949: Filippo De Pisis's[8] triptych *Parigi*, *Piazza con le palme*, and *Tra porto e marina*, a rural landscape by the impressionist Arturo Tosi[9] and the pair of pictures *Dedalo e Icaro* and *Giovanetto e Fauno* by Odoardo Vicinelli,[10] an artist of the neoclassical period. The taste displayed by the young collector Mattei was a very generic one, but over the years it grew more selective and oriented toward contemporary art, as is demonstrated by the acquisitions he made in 1950–51: *Veduta di Venezia* (n.d.) and *Omaggio a Fattori* (1933) by De Pisis,[11] *Case di Zoppè (Cadore)* by Tomea,[12] *Paesaggio della Val Seriana* (circa 1940) by Tosi,[13] several works by Chighine,[14] Breveglieri,[15] and Rosai[16] and two still lifes by Morandi,[17] painted between 1919 and 1941. These purchases were made well before 1952 and are a tangible sign and proof of the fact that, on his walks with Grossetti, Mattei was anything but a novice where art was concerned.[18]

The artistic education of the entrepreneur from Matelica can very probably be traced back to his friendship with Marcello Boldrini. Professor of statistics at the Catholic University in Milan, from the same town as Mattei and like him a resident of Via Fatebenefratelli, Boldrini introduced the young industrialist to the future leaders of the Christian Democrats (De Gasperi, Fanfani, La Pira, Dossetti). From 1943 onward Mattei had made the preparations for his activity in the years of the Resistance at Boldrini's home, where he had long conversations with Marcello's wife, Renata Boldrini, a great lover of art. Mattei would come to rely on Renata[19] as a sort of personal artistic advisor not just for his own purchases but also in matters of design and advertising. When, in April 1952, a competition was announced in the magazine *Domus* to choose the trademarks of the Supercortemaggiore and Agipgas products, Renata Boldrini, along with the director of public relations Luigi Faleschini, was called on to represent AGIP on the panel of judges. The jury had some prestigious members: among others, the painter Mario Sironi, the engraver Mino Maccari and the architect Gio Ponti. This gives us an indication of the high regard in which Mattei held his own adviser on art, who would play a part in the selection of the winner of the section devoted to poster design for Supercortemaggiore, Luigi Broggini's famous six-legged dog.[20]

The competition notice of 1952 brings us back to Via dell'Annunciata in Milan. According to Grossetti it was Mattei (perhaps on the advice of Renata Boldrini) who came up with the idea of exhibiting some of the over 4000 designs submitted to the competition but not selected among the winners. If for no other reason than to draw attention to the work of distinguished artists who had taken part—including Fortunato Depero, Armando Testa and Marcello Nizzoli—and had taken their exclusion badly.[21] This somewhat unusual idea was received favorably by the director of the Annunciata, who made the spaces of his gallery available for the show. "I accepted the unusual proposal with pleasure," recalled the gallery owner, "and the original paintings occupied the whole place, hung in three rows, filling the walls of the bar, the gallery and the room upstairs and giving the premises a bizarre appearance."[22] In addition to the numerous works of art acquired for **eni**, Mattei personally bought a number of pictures for his private collection, which was put up for auction at Christie's in 2002 (lots 287–327).[23] From both groups of works emerges the portrait of a man of great curiosity, ready to travel in search of his artists, going to Rome, Milan, Venice (Galleria del Cavallino), Turin (Galleria La Nuova Bussola) and even outside the country. He undoubtedly had a preference for Tosi, Tomea, De Pisis, Carrà, Morandi and Cantatore, but was also capable of making bold choices, "outside the mold," like Sironi's *Cantiere* and *Composizioni*,[24] Casorati's *Nudo disteso che legge*[25] (n.d.) (both from the Annunciata) or Picasso's *Le combat de centaures*,[26] an ink on paper of 1946, bought at the Galerie Leiris in Paris. There are also some very intimate reasons at the root of Mattei's artistic preferences. Both the **eni** collection and the private one are dominated by landscapes filled with trees that reminded him of the countryside around Matelica and by views of the mountains that took him back to his summer trips to the Dolomites, in the region of Cadore. There are many still lifes—whether in the realistic versions of Tosi and Tomea or in the symbolistic ones of Carrà and Morandi—that reflect Mattei's introverted and meditative character and his passion for the pragmatism of real life. Even the portraits of women belong to the realm of introspective contemplation, sometimes in the maternal (Cantatore) and sensual sphere (Guttuso and Casorati), at others in an abstract one (Birolli and Cassinari). In particular the meditative-contemplative aspect lies behind Mattei's absolute preference for the work of De Pisis, as is suggested by a significant episode recounted by Fiorenea Giacobbe: "In Mattei a man full of faith in human powers and values coexisted with a man who was dramatically alone. In his study he had a picture by De Pisis [*Omaggio a Fattori*, 1933, N/A], a marvelous pale blue ground standing out diagonally from a gray wall; under the wall, a small bundle of rags that could be a man, the outline of a man... One morning I was about to enter and the president didn't hear me: he was standing with his eyes fixed on the picture, slowly shaking his head... he was moved. The day after I replaced the picture; I didn't think that it brought a smile to his face. The president asked why I had taken it down. He said to me: 'Don't you see that that little man of rags is me?'" Along with painting on canvas, Mattei displayed a high degree of artistic understanding of the fields of lithography, as is demonstrated by his acquisition of Capogrossi's *Superficie 150* (1956),[27] and sculpture, represented by artists like Aldo Caron,[28] Pericle Fazzini[29] and Eugenio Tomiolo.[30]

From 1959 onward Mattei combined his activity as a collector of works for his own houses or the company offices with that of a promoter of art in Italy and abroad. The area he focused on inside the country's borders was the Marche, the region of Mattei's birth.[31] For this reason the request for funding for the Premio Marche by Francesco Angelini, mayor of Ancona, was received favorably by the president's office for three years in a row, up until 1962, with the company allocating a total of 300 thousand lire.[32] The area of Abruzzo—where his father Antonio had worked in the times of the brigand Musolino—also attracted Mattei's interest, prompting him to gather information on the Premio di Avezzano[33] and the Premio Valle Roveto, in which the young Cesco Magnolato, launched by the exhibition at the Permanente, would win first prize. Another initiative that can be linked with Mattei is the institution of the Premio Sicilia Industria within the context of the industrial revival of the island that was supposed to be kick-started by the construction of the petrochemical refinery at Gela.[34]

In 1959 the internationalization of the company—now on a significant scale following the signing of contracts with Egypt, Iran and Tunisia—started to have repercussions on its promotion of art as well. This explains the contribution of about 500 thousand lire to the Istituto Italiano per l'Africa on the occasion of the Second World

Congress of Black Writers and Artists,[35] which saw the participation of a number of artists who later became famous, such as the South African Gerard Sekoto and the Ghanaian Kofi Antubam.

Also decisive—to this idea of a wide-ranging promotion of art—was Mattei's meeting with Vittore Querel, director of the Galleria La Feluca in Rome and chair of the Briefing Conference on Contemporary Arab Art and Italo-Arab Artistic Relations. Querel offered Mattei a seat on the advisory board of the conference and within a few months received a substantial donation for the eighth Premio San Vito Romano.[36] This was about a year after that July 25, 1961, when the OAS threatened to kill the president of **eni** if he continued his political campaign in support of the Algerian National Liberation Front. But Mattei's response to those threats was an ever deeper commitment—on the cultural level as well—to the improvement of relations with Africa and the Middle East.

One little studied aspect of Mattei's patronage regards the promotion of artistic culture within the companies of the **eni** group through a series of awards and art exhibitions devoted to employees. Mattei was aware that creating opportunities and spaces for the cultivation of artistic talent meant strengthening the sense of corporate identity and belonging. In February 1956 SNAM staged the first Premio per le arti figurative ("Prize for the Figurative Arts")[37] at the Galleria Apollinaire of Milan, which was to continue throughout Boldrini's presidency. Shortly afterward, in 1960, it was the turn of ANIC in Ravenna to open an exhibition of its own in the presence of the minister Benigno Zaccagnini.[38] Similar initiatives were often organized "from below" by the employees themselves, as in the case of the exhibition of paintings in 1958 at Rome's Istituto Angelicum, in the Dominican cloister of Santa Maria sopra Minerva.[39] The monthly feature entitled *I pittori della domenica* ["The Sunday Painters"] in the magazine *Il Gatto Selvatico* edited by the poet, journalist and art critic Attilio Bertolucci was also dedicated to employees. It was Bertolucci, for instance, who had the idea of entrusting the opening of each issue to an artist, the engraver Mino Maccari, and of closing the magazine with a column of lessons of art history, ranging from the classics to the historic avant-gardes and contemporary currents. The editor and poet also devoted particular attention to publishing reports on major international artistic events, such as the Venice Biennale or the Milan Triennale, written by established critics like Marco Valsecchi and Roberto Longhi.

To understand Mattei's interest in the world of the figurative arts it is necessary to place his activity as a patron in a precise sociocultural context. The period from the early fifties to the mid-sixties marked the rise of a ruling and industrial class open to change. Enlightened entrepreneurship saw in the alliance between the worlds of art and industry, something that a number of intellectuals were also calling for, a concrete possibility of steering the transformation of society in a certain direction; a society that risked, if unprepared, being overwhelmed by the shockwave of development and technological progress. The first oil company to set up an award for young artists was Esso Italia, with the competition *Il Petrolio e l'Industria* ["Oil and the Oil Industry"] staged by *Esso Rivista* in 1951 at the Galleria di Roma and held three more times, up until 1962, with the collaboration of figures like Giuliano Briganti and Lionello Venturi. From Turin came news of the Picassos and Modiglianis bought by Giovanni Agnelli. This was echoed at Ivrea by the initiatives of Adriano Olivetti, who after founding the magazine *Comunità* (1946) organized two one-man shows devoted to Licini and Casorati, as well as promoting industrial architecture through the magazine *SeleArte*, edited by Carlo Ludovico Ragghianti. Shortly afterward (1953) Leonardo Sinisgalli would launch, under the guidance of the new general manager of Finmeccanica Giuseppe Eugenio Luraghi, the magazine *Civiltà delle macchine*, which became one of the most important points of reference in the debate between business and culture. Thanks in part to Sinisgalli's suggestions, Alberto Pirelli commissioned from Renato Guttuso a mosaic entitled *Ricerca Scientifica* in Milan, while

Benzine

agipgas

promoting in the *Rivista Pirelli* the "Pittori in Fabbrica" ["Painters in the Factory"] initiative, dedicated to talented employees.

After Mattei's death the large deficit from which the company had suffered since 1961 obliged his successors to cut back the plans of artistic promotion, without completely forgetting the lesson of its founder. Marcello Boldrini, appointed president of **eni** following the tragedy of the plane crash at Bascapè, was a man with a wide range of interests. He wrote an article for *Il Gatto Selvatico* describing in great detail the exhibition in Milan devoted to the International Gothic in Lombardy. In 1965, at Parma Baptistery and in the presence of the critic Roberto Longhi, he presented Attilio Bertolucci's work on the Romanesque art of the Po Valley, made with the financial support of the company.[40] The relations with galleries and major exhibitions continued, as is evident from the correspondence with the Galleria Il Punto in Palermo, where Guttuso showed,[41] with Vittore Querel's La Feluca and the Galleria San Marco in Rome,[42] or with La Pira, who invited Boldrini to the opening of the exhibition in Florence devoted to Le Corbusier.[43] However, these contacts did not always lead to the hoped-for funding or acquisitions. On more than one occasion requests for contributions to exhibitions[44] or allowances for emerging artists or those seeking success were turned down.[45] A number of purchases were blocked, in some cases stirring great controversy.[46] Yet the guiding thread of corporate patronage was not broken thanks to the presence of Renata Boldrini—Mattei's former personal adviser—who suggested the acquisition of works by a number of prominent artists like De Luigi and Perez.

There was a halt in acquisitions during the presidency of Eugenio Cefis[47] (1967–71), when the company's patronage was channeled into the promotion and financial support of exhibitions—in particular "Roma Neoclassica"[48]—and international conferences. Especially important was the relationship established between Cefis and Luigi Preti, Socialist member of parliament and future minister of finance and economic planning (1969). In 1968 Preti interceded on behalf of the Convegno Internazionale Artisti, Critici e Studiosi d'Arte in Rimini, describing Cefis's financial assistance as an "enlightened example of understanding and generosity."[49] The sponsorship and funding of 250 thousand lire—which rose to 650 thousand in 1969 and to 1 million in 1970—was accompanied by Cefis's granting of funding for the two-year period 1970–71 for the Centro Pio Manzù in Verucchio, headed by Preti himself.

The purchase of works of art was resumed under the presidencies of Raffaele Girotti (1971–75) and Pietro Sette (1975–79). It was during this period that a number of pictures of great significance entered the collection, such as Casorati's *Ritratto di signora* (n.d.),[50] Sironi's *Due figure* (1950),[51] and more works by Rosai, Cassinari and Mafai. With the exception of Tosi and Tomea—who were Mattei's personal choices—it is possible that behind these acquisitions was again the figure of Renata Boldrini, officially reinstated as artistic adviser during Sette's presidency.[52] This would explain the absolute adherence to Mattei's catalogue in the choice of painters and sculptors. Girotti was also responsible for the attempt to reestablish the contacts with the world of Arab artist forged by Mattei, as is demonstrated by the correspondence with Salah Kamel, ambassador of Egyptian culture in the years of the UAR,[53] on the occasion of the Venice Biennale in 1970.[54]

The period from 1979 to 1982—which coincided with the second oil crisis—was marked by disappointing economic returns and a rapid rotation of top management. Yet even at such a complicated moment there were some noteworthy operations linked to the names of Enrico Gandolfi and Umberto Colombo for the corporate acquisitions and Bruno Cimino, Giuseppe Faverzani and Marcello Colitti for those made by AGIP. It suffices to think that in 1982 alone a total of sixty works entered the collection: these included artists already represented in

Mattei's time—such as Guttuso (*Paesaggio predesertico*, circa 1978)[55] and Cassinari (*Ritratto antico*, n.d.)[56]—while other artists of international renown made their first appearance, including Giacomo Manzù, Fabrizio Clerici, Salvatore Fiume and Enrico Castellani. Then there were works signed by Luigi Boille, Renzo Vespignani and Giovanni Cappelli, present in the catalogue of the Permanente in 1958. It almost seemed to be the closing of a circle, but it was not so.

For the company founded by Mattei the nineties were a time of great change: from the privatization begun in 1992 to the listing on the stock exchange in 1995 and the process of breaking up the company into divisions, which commenced in 1998. It was a tumultuous period in many ways, which saw the company embark on a highly innovative phase of cultural and artistic experimentation. The spirit that drove the top managers of that time—Gabriele Cagliari, Raffaele Santoro, Guglielmo Moscato and Alberto Meomartini—ushered in a period of "progressive patronage" comparable to the one imagined by Mattei. An example is the "Finesecolo" project of 1991—recently called to mind by da Sandro Fusina[57]—carried out in collaboration with the Circolo San Fedele. The plan was that for ten years—until the end of the century and the millennium—**eni**, AGIP and SNAM would buy a certain number of works produced by Italian artists over the course of the year, with the aim of documenting the entire panorama of Italian production. In the first year twenty-four works of great importance were chosen and purchased—including Valerio Adami's *Tavola e città* (1991),[58] Alighiero Boetti's *Aeroplani* (1990)[59] and Stefano Arienti's *Senza titolo* (n.d.)[60]—many of them by artists who now enjoyed an established reputation (like Mimmo Rotella or Salvatore Scarpitta).[61]

To some extent **eni**'s involvement in the promotion of art followed the increasingly global dimension of the company, with the acquisition of a series of works by foreign painters and sculptors alongside Italian ones. Among them were Eugeniusz Eibisch,[62] a painter and illustrator from Kraków; Hussein el Gebali,[63] one of the most important Egyptian lithographers; Marcel Gotène, a first-rate Congolese painter; Hsiao Chin,[64] a Chinese artist of exceptional talent and friend of Fontana, Manzoni and Burri. Into this complex picture can be fitted the relationship established in 1991 between Meomartini's SNAM and the Belgian artist Jean-Michel Folon for a series of advertising campaigns—launched with the celebrated slogan "Methane gives you a hand"—that made some of his works (like *Uomo con le fiammelle*, n.d., or *Uomo che guarda il tramonto*, 1998, two out of a total of sixty watercolors) genuine icons of an era.[65] Among the more significant operations linked to the world of art, a truly momentous passage was marked by the restoration of the façade of St. Peter's Basilica to coincide with the Jubilee of 2000,[66] on which work started in 1996, during the Moscato presidency, and which was unveiled by John Paul II[67] on September 30, 1999. The success of the initiative was such as to persuade the company to undertake a similar project, at the request of the local authorities, for the restoration of the façade of Milan Duomo in 2003.[68]

In recent years, as a consequence of the growing interest in the question of sustainability, the attitude of major companies to the relationship with the world of the cultural heritage has changed considerably. From interventions of sponsorship linked to the occasional financing of exhibitions, restorations and publications the emphasis has increasingly shifted to actions that reflect the company's awareness of its responsibility to society and the territory. The key word is partnership, a more active, dynamic and conscious vision of the relationship between business and culture, which finds expression in a series of initiatives aimed at in-depth study of the cultural heritage and making it freely accessible. It is in this context that we should set the initiatives in support of art which have seen the company play a leading role, focusing on the rediscovery of the great masters of the history of art and the presentation of a number of little known masterpieces to the public. Betwe-

en 2006 and 2007 **eni** was the main sponsor of an exhibition devote to Mantegna in Mantua, the city where a few months later it promoted the exhibition "La forza del bello" at Palazzo Te, made up of over a hundred works of classical Greek art. In 2008, in collaboration with the Museo d'Arte Moderna in Bologna, it exhibited two works by Morandi (*Natura morta*, 1919, and *Natura morta con bottiglie*, 1941) at a retrospective of the artist at the Metropolitan Museum of Art in New York. From the same year dates the prestigious partnership with the Musée du Louvre, with the monographic exhibition on Mantegna, and with another exhibition in Paris on Titian, Tintoretto and Veronese in 2009. The agreement with the Louvre also permitted the exhibition of Leonardo's *Saint John the Baptist* (1508–13) in Milan (2009) and Rome (2010), attracting a record number of visitors. The formula of putting a single work on display free of charge—accompanied by personalized guided tours and a broad range of initiatives (distribution of informative material, catalogues, dedicated website)—had already been tried out in 2008 with the exhibition of Caravaggio's *Conversion of Saul* (1600–01) in Milan, followed up by a successful replica of the undertaking at Porto Ercole. Over the last two years **eni** has also formed partnerships with the Palais des Beaux-Arts in Brussels on the occasion of the exhibition "From van Dyck to Bellotto" and with the museum activities of the Fondazione Musei Civici di Venezia (which comprises, among others, Palazzo Ducale, Museo Correr, Torre dell'Orologio and Ca' Rezzonico). Separate mention must be made of the set of collaborations (with the Monument to Vittorio Emanuele II and the Casa d'Arte Futurista Depero) linked to the traveling exhibition "Il cane a sei zampe" ("The Six-Legged Dog") that has made it possible to retrace—through images, original documents, TV spots, memorabilia and satirical cartoons drawn from the rich resources of the **eni** historical archives and from private collections—the history of the trademark designed by Luigi Broggini, which also represented a turning point in the commercial art of those years. What seems to emerge from this overall picture in the last few years is a clear shift away from the example of Mattei and his successors, who had made the support of emerging talents a sort of banner. Yet this impression is belied by **eni**'s latest advertising campaign in which it has chosen to take a precise approach, espousing without reservations the elective affinities with art and multimedia design, a category of creativity that is open to all possible avant-garde languages. And out of this **eni** decided to commit its communication to a hothouse of culturally versatile artists, sought out and selected all over the world, with a well-considered DNA: talent, multimedia dynamism, search for the new. From February 2010 to today the number of such talents uncovered and already at work on advertising campaigns and projects of institutional communication is over forty, coming from Europe, Asia, Africa and America.

What emerges clearly from this brief overview of the relationship with art is a strong thread binding the present to the past. Just as with other values that **eni** carries in its genetic makeup and culture, the attention paid to art, with an attitude that is not one of mere patronage but dynamic and interlocutory, is an integral part of the way in which this company relates to the territory and to people.

This essay was written to mark the completion of the new cataloguing of **eni**'s artistic patrimony in 2009. In the six volumes of the catalogue can be found, for each entry, a detailed description of the work and its author, a text setting the artistic movement to which it belongs in its historical context, an appendix on its provenance and a bibliography.

1 The building, constructed by Luca Beltrami, one of the greatest Milanese architects of the time of Umberto I, had been reconstructed in 1953 by Achille Castiglioni, who had turned it into the seat of the National Biennial of Art.
2 Cf. *Giovani artisti italiani: Milano, 20 aprile-16 maggio*. Milan: SEL, 1958. On the exhibition and Enrico Mattei's relationship with the art world see G. Accorinti, *Quando Mattei era l'impresa energetica. Io c'ero*. Matelica: Hacca-Halley, 2007², pp. 90–91.
3 From the article published in *Il Giorno* (Sunday May 11, 1958) we know that the opening was attended by some of the most prominent figures in Milanese culture: the journalist Carla Ravaioli, the art dealer Alfredo Bonino and the director of the Galleria Montenapoleone, Serena Perfetti.
4 An art critic, university professor, essayist and journalist for *Il Giorno* and *Il Giornale*, he was a contributor to the magazine *Il Gatto Selvatico* in 1956. Along with his colleagues Gaetano Baldacci and Sirio Musso, he was a member of the executive committee of the exhibition at the Permanente.
5 B. Grossetti, *Il mercante dell'Annunciata. Confessioni e memorie*. Milan: Mazzotta, 1958, p. 60.
6 Archivio Storico **eni** (hereafter ASE), Fonti Orali, "Intervista a Fiorenea Giacobbe," pp. 7–8.
7 G. Accorinti, op. cit., p. 90.
8 *Catalogo del patrimonio artistico eni* (hereafter *PAE*). Rome: Iniziative culturali **eni**, 2010, vol. I, pp. 340–60.
9 *PAE*, III, p. 1298.

10 *PAE*, III, pp. 1404–07.
11 *PAE* I, Iniziative culturali **eni**, Rome 2010, p. 388.
12 *PAE*, I, p. 398. At the request of Mattei Tomea he also realized the famous mosaic in the apse of the church of Santa Barbara at San Donato in 1959, cf. G. Accorinti, op. cit., p. 93; *Il Gatto Selvatico* (hereafter *GS*), March 1959, p. 24.
13 *PAE*, III, p. 1304.
14 *PAE*, I, pp. 115–18.
15 *PAE*, I, pp. 257–65.
16 *PAE*, III, pp. 1071–83.
17 *PAE*, II, pp. 932–40.
18 Fiorenea Giacobbe recounts that "he happily browsed through Giotto and Masaccio; but I think that the period of painting he preferred was that of the impressionists." Cf. ASE, Fonti Orali, "Intervista a Fiorenea Giacobbe," pp. 7–8.
19 G. Accorinti, op. cit., p. 74. According to Fiorenea Giacobbe we should not forget the influence exercised on Mattei by Orfeo Tamburi, a painter from the Marche who had "a considerable sway over his choices in the field of art."
20 L. Nardi, "La vera storia del cane a sei zampe," in *Il cane a sei zampe*. Rome: **eni**, 2009, pp. 10–17.
21 L. Nardi, op. cit., p. 14
22 B. Grossetti, op. cit., p. 60.
23 *Christie's Contemporary - Evening Sale: Wednesday 6 February - Day Sale: Friday 8 February* (hereafter *Christie's*), Milan–Rome 2002, pp. 108–25. On the auction see G. Accorinti, op. cit., p. 90; on Mattei's private collection see the article by P. Manazza, "Il bello di Enrico Mattei," in *Corriere Economia*, May 1, 2000, p. 13.
24 *Christie's*, p. 113, *PAE*, III, pp. 1186 and 1196.
25 *Christie's*, pp. 118–19
26 *Christie's*, pp. 111. On the picture see too C. Zervos, *Pablo Picasso*. Paris: Editions Cahiers d'Art, 1963, vol. 14, no. 222.

27 Capogrossi was an exponent of the Roman School and a figure of considerable importance in the panorama of Italian nonrepresentational painting, along with artists like Lucio Fontana, Alberto Burri and Emilio Scanavino.
28 *PAE*, VI, pp. 46–49. *GS*, October 1958, p. 26; *GS*, October 1960, p. 11–12; *GS*, October 1961, p. 14; G. Accorinti, op. cit., p. 94. Giorgio Dal Bosco tells us that Mattei met Caron on August 15, 1954. On the death of Alcide De Gasperi, Caron was asked to make a cast of his face by Ezio Vanoni (cf. G. Dal Bosco, "La spalla dolorante del ministro e l'artista caustico," in *Trentino*, August 15, 2008, p. 53).
29 *PAE*, VI, p. 69. *GS*, November 1958; *GS*, March 1960, pp. 14–16; *GS*, December 1961, p. 17.
30 *PAE*, VI, p. 126. The competition notice in *Domus* (cf. L. Nardi, op. cit., p. 16) tells us that Eugenio Tomiolo's design was awarded second prize in the Supercortemaggiore poster section, won by Broggini's six-legged dog.
31 It is likely that a push in the direction of the promotion of the art of the Marche came from Mattei's participation in the exhibition *Pittori romani e marchigiani* that opened in Rome on March 25, 1959, cf. ASE, **eni**, Organi Sociali, "Presidenza Enrico Mattei," b. 85, fasc. 630.
32 ASE, **eni**, Organi Sociali, "Presidenza Enrico Mattei," b. 65, fasc. D43.
33 ASE, **eni**, Organi Sociali, "Presidenza Enrico Mattei," b. 30, fasc. 6B6.
34 Among the papers of Boldrini's secretary's office there is one referring to Mattei's explicit support for the grant, through Agip Mineraria, of a sum of 150 thousand lire to the Istituto per lo Sviluppo Iniziative in Sicilia (ISIS) to be used as a prize for the winner, the painter Enzo Brunori. See ASE, **eni**, Organi Sociali, "Presidenza Enrico Mattei," b. 2, fasc. 4D3.
35 ASE, **eni**, Relazioni Esterne, "Relazioni pubbliche," b. 87, fasc. 2E3F.

36 ASE, **eni**, Relazioni Esterne, "Relazioni pubbliche," b. 1, fasc. 4D2. On October 26, 1962, the day before the tragedy at Bascapè, Mattei sent a contribution of 500 thousand lire to Querel.

37 *GS*, November-December 1956, p. 28.

38 *GS*, June 1958, pp. 13–14.

39 *GS*, July 1960, pp. 31–32.

40 Archivio Cinematografico **eni**, "Cinegiornali Sedi 1963-1965," no. D10.

41 ASE, **eni**, Organi Sociali, "Presidenza Enrico Mattei," b. 63, fasc. CA6.

42 ASE, **eni**, Organi Sociali, "Presidenza Enrico Mattei," b. 2, fasc. 4D3.

43 In 1964 Derna and Vittore Querel invited Boldrini to attend the opening of an exhibition by ?Ruth?, a Californian painter appreciated by some important collectors, like Paul Getty. See ASE, **eni**, Organi Sociali, "Presidenza Enrico Mattei," b. 1, fasc. 4D2. The same year he was invited to the solo exhibition of Olga Grandi Dall'Orto.

44 In 1964 Padre Guidubaldi, editor of the art magazine *Europa Oggi*, requested funding of 500 dollars for an exhibition in New York on the macchiaioli. The sum, to be allocated "essentially as a form of industrial patronage, in exchange for publicity," was perhaps the first modern call for sponsorship in the history of **eni**.

45 See the case of the painter Mario Morigi from Romagna, recommended by the member of parliament Arrigo Righi, or that of the sculptor Alfio Castelli from the Marche, who had the support of the minister Giuseppe Medici.

46 This is what happened with the failure to buy Arnaldo Pomodoro's *Traveler's Column*, initially promised by Boldrini to Giovanni Carandente, to be erected at the Motel Agip in Spoleto. Cf. ASE, **eni**, Organi sociali, "Presidenza Enrico Mattei," b. 63, fasc. C97.

47 However, even under the Cefis presidency funding for figurative art did not dry up, as is demonstrated by **eni**'s contributions to the Centro Internazionale Artisti Critici Studiosi d'Arte di Verucchio and the Centro Pio Manzù, supported by the Honorable Luigi Preti (ASE, **eni**, Organi sociali, "Presidenza Eugenio Cefis," b. 18 fasc. 7E1; ASE, **eni**, Relazioni esterne, "Relazioni pubbliche," b. 7, fasc. 218B).

48 ASE, **eni**, Organi sociali, "Presidenza Eugenio Cefis," b. 13, fasc. 542.

49 ASE, **eni**, Relazioni esterne, "Relazioni pubbliche," b. 7, fasc. 218B.

50 *PAE*, I, p. 218.

51 *PAE*, III, p. 1191.

52 In a letter (Cat. **eni**, 456—Vicinelli) of December 23, 1975, Renata Boldrini provided a biographical entry on the artist, indicating the literature available, and an estimate of the value of the collection.

53 United Arab Republic (UAR) was the name of the state created by the political union of Syria and Egypt, which would later be joined, in a more elastic confederation, by North Yemen. Even after Syria's secession in 1961, Egypt continued to use the name until December 31, 1971.

54 ASE, **eni**, Organi sociali, "Presidenza Eugenio Cefis," b. 255, fasc. 47D8.

55 *PAE*, II, p. 778.

56 *PAE*, I, p. 227.

57 S. Fusina, "Mecenate da sempre. L'impegno di Eni per l'arte risale ai tempi del Giorno di Enrico Mattei," in *Il Foglio*, November 28, 2009, p. 4.

58 *PAE*, I, p. 9.

59 *PAE*, I, p. 78.

60 *PAE*, I, p. 19.

61 *PAE*, III, p. 1088 and *PAE*, VI, p. 104. Rotella and Scarpitta had also been "launched" by Mattei in 1958 in the exhibition at the Permanente. The members of the buying commission included some of the most prestigious authorities of the time, such as Augusta Monferrina, director of the Galleria Nazionale d'Arte Moderna, and Pier Giovanni Castagnola, director of the Galleria d'Arte Moderna in Modena. The project—as a consequence of a series of problems within the company—did not get beyond the first year. Cf. S. Fusina, op. cit., p. 4.

62 *PAE*, I, p. 450.

63 *PAE*, IV, p. 250.

64 *PAE*, I, p. 273.

65 ASE, Snam, Programmazione metano, "Attività pubblicitaria," b. 1, fascc. 9DA-9D9. In 1997 SNAM decided to buy thirty-nine works by Folon, who for his part donated the sculpture *Uomo con le fiammelle*, now in the hall of the first **eni** Office Building at San Donato Milanese. *PAE*, II, pp. 492–696.

66 L. Accattoli, "Un super restauro per la Basilica di San Pietro: paga l'Eni," in *Il Corriere della sera*, February 28, 1997, p. 13. The restoration of St. Peter's is often cited as the first case of cause-related marketing. On this see D. Viglione, "La fabbrica di San Pietro, progetto di restauro e conservazione," in D. Pitteri, S. Picucci and R.M. Villani, *Cause Related Marketing. Agire competitivo dell'impresa e nuovo Mercato*. Milan: Franco Angeli, 2002, pp. 129–34.

67 S. Lorusso, "Osservazioni sul progetto di restauro della Facciata della Basilica di San Pietro, realizzato a cura della Fabbrica di San Pietro con il supporto scientifico dell'Eni," in *Restauro della Facciata della Basilica di San Pietro: l'apporto di EniTecnologie*, proceedings of the conference (Rome, December 9, 1999). Rome: 2000, pp. 51–59. The project has recently been extended over the period from 2009 to 2013 to cover the colonnade too. Cf. C. Barnini, "Al via per San Pietro. In piazza San Pietro il colonnato tornerà all'antico splendore," in *Giornale Roma*, April 23, 2010, p. 45.

68 B. Mörlin Visconti Castiglione, "Operazione Duomo," in *Eni's Way*, 1 (2003), pp. 74–79.

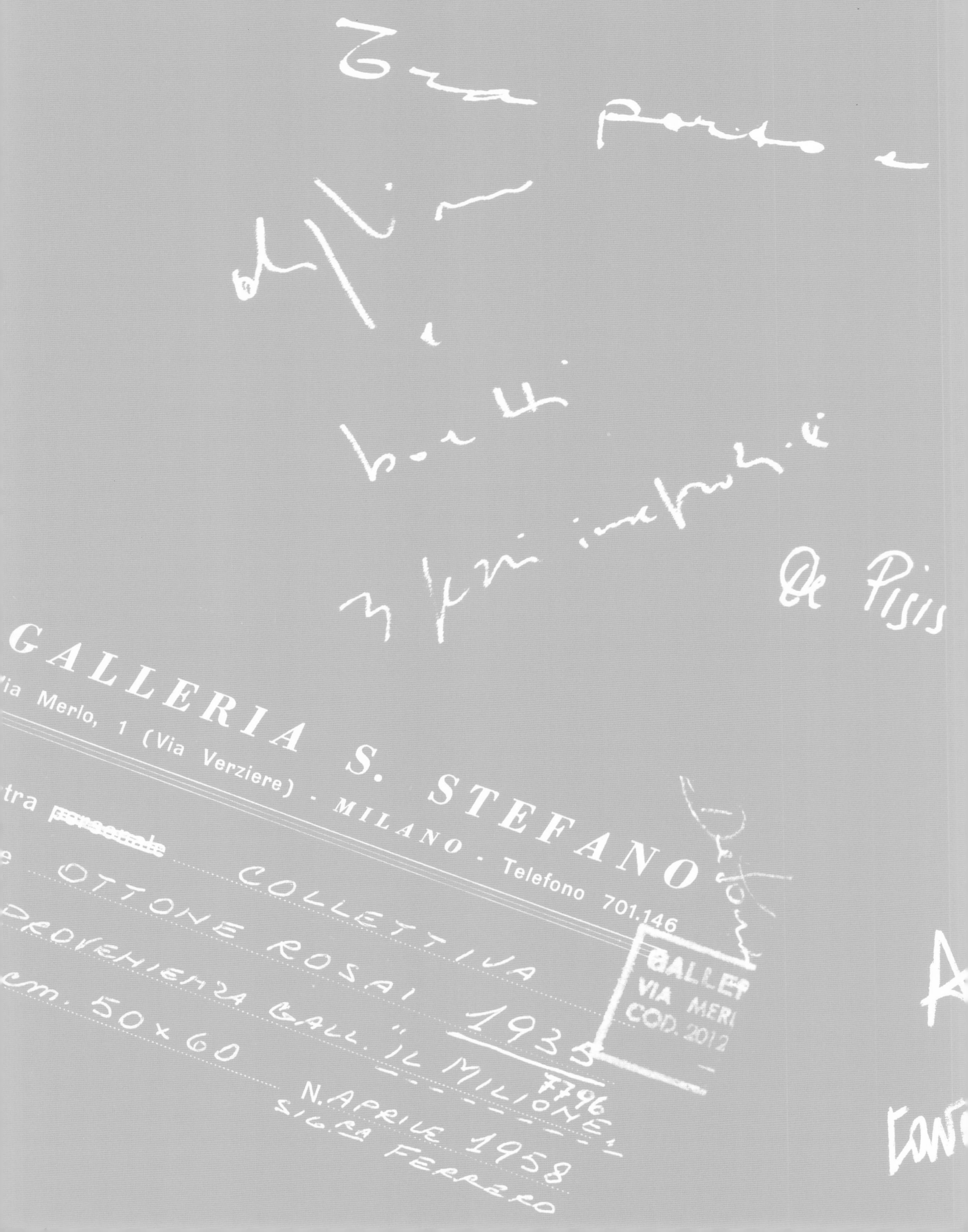

De Pisis
GALLERIA S. STEFANO
Via Merlo, 1 (Via Verziere) - MILANO - Telefono 701.146
COLLETTIVA
OTTONE ROSAI
1935
PROVENIENZA GALL. "IL MILIONE"
cm. 50 × 60
7796
N. APRILE 1958
SIG.RA FERRERO
VIA MERI
COD. 2012

italian 20th-century art

Cinzia Chiari
*Responsible for the cataloguing of **eni**'s art collections*

eni's art collection and its new cataloguing

The figurative bias of the collection, which was certainly there from the outset, has been reinforced over the years both in an effort to counter pressing theses of abstraction and out of a conviction of the need for a concrete language amidst the ever growing vacuity of social and cultural values. The image retains its strong existential content, but is intensified in its essence of immediacy and recognizability. Part of this comes from the experience gained in the realization of the public monument, where perspective and distance of the point of view require greater characterization of visibility; part from the professional determination that considers the solution of the work to take priority over the solicitation of suggestions and injections of emotional meaning; and part from the desire of Mattei, a collector sensitive to beauty and abreast of the times.
Claudio Rizzi

Following the guidelines laid down by its founder, Enrico Mattei, **eni** has displayed from the very first years of its life a strong sense of social responsibility toward its own country and toward the foreign countries in which it has operated. A sense of responsibility that has grown over the years and that has imposed a company policy attentive to the needs of its workers, its customers, the territory in which it is acting and, more in general, the culture and system of values that are conveyed through its communication.

If the idea of an art collection was initially an expression of Enrico Mattei's personal desire and then a simple, and sometimes fortuitous, accumulation of works and objects, this does not mean that it is not possible to find in all this a *raison d'être* that goes beyond the simple fact of its existence. The **eni** art collection is in fact the tangible sign of a cultural need felt in an original way by a company whose impact on the country goes well beyond the industrial one and that has come to define itself as a symbol of the Italian spirit, presented and perceived all over the world as such.

But there is more: this collection is a fruit of the expansion of international relations over the decades, almost as if the work of art, in an interminable series of exchanges of technologies and skills between countries, could be the best means of sealing industrial relations and then partnerships and finally friendships. Thus not only does the collection, to a great extent, offer a cross-section of the history of Italian art since the last war, including the work of its greatest masters, but it is also a sort of symbolic map on which to draw and measure the growth of a company in the world, its contacts and its relations.

Although scattered over the company's many offices and branches the **eni** art collection is therefore a single entity. Jurists would say that it has the quality of a *universitas rerum*, i.e. an aggregate of things whose value is increased by being part of a whole. The splendid works of Folon, for example, would in fact be less significant if in addition to their intrinsic artistic value they were not also the memento of many years of cutting-edge publicity, occupying a space somewhere between industry and art, that the company had programed in a far-sighted way, often anticipating future fashions. And if they were not also a heritage on which to draw or against which to gauge new advertising campaigns.

But precisely because of its diffuse nature, this art collection needed a new cataloguing that would be able to communicate the unitary sense of hundreds of paintings, sculptures, objets d'art, pieces of furniture and carpets, of different values, origins and periods. A cataloguing that in the first place would act as a repertory of images and then as a register of values. But which could also provide guidance for a future exploitation or for a further campaign of acquisitions.

Exploitation is in fact the logical consequence of a cataloguing that must not remain a dead letter, but become a tool with which to plan interventions to increase the value and substance of a heritage that has been found to be more solid than was estimated prior to this work. Exploitation can also entail making loans to international cultural institutions and participation in various projects realized with numerous museums in Italy and in the rest of the world. However, cataloguing is also an opportunity to study the history of art more deeply, naturally taking it all the way up to contemporaneity, through works that reflect the history and identity of **eni**, and the cultural policy that it has adopted over the years. Finally, it should not be forgotten that a good cataloguing is also the first step toward good conservation, as it provides an accurate picture of the condition of the works at a particular moment, giving us the possibility of gauging their state of preservation and planning restorations where necessary.

But the **eni** collection also obliges us to make a more general digression on collecting, since one of the most engaging aspects of the work of art is that it is a unique, unrepeatable phenomenon, a single object that often becomes a fetish and whose significance is also enhanced by the fact that it "belongs" to a given collection. So much so that collecting represents an important aspect of the art world itself and it is precisely collecting that creates a status which in the case of some large companies can almost become a branch of its activity, a parallel aspect to the main one that it uses to give itself an image and to communicate it.

And there are many cases of collecting by "major companies" that, although with different intentions and interests, have assembled hundreds and sometimes thousands of works of art retracing their own history, devoting themselves to their territory of origin or to a historical period particularly connected with the history of the company, and even expressing the maximum freedom, dependent on the circumstances.

For example the Unicredit Collection, which is made up of the separate art collections of the individual banks that have joined the group following mergers and takeovers, is now one of the richest corporate collections in Europe, with around 60,000 works, ranging from archeological finds from Mesopotamia to works by the great masters of the past and examples of contemporary art.

Or the Würth Collection, commenced in the sixties by Reinhold Würth, which comprises art works of the 20th and 21st centuries. In recent times it has been expanded through the acquisition of one of the most important collections of 15th- and 16th-century German and Swiss painting, the one that used to belong to the princes of Fürstenberg. Today the collection contains over 12,500 works of painting, graphic art and sculpture.

Or again the collection of the Banca Monte dei Paschi di Siena that, in addition to being the result of a systematic project of relatively recent origin, is also the product of centuries of commissions and acquisitions that have gradually assumed the character of a genuine collection. The earliest works of art were realized to bring prestige and fame to the bank at the moment of its creation and during the significant episodes of its activity since the outset. It suffices to think that in 1481, to celebrate the foundation of the Monte di Pietà, as the institution was originally known, in 1472, Benvenuto di Giovanni del Guasta was commissioned to paint the fresco of the *Madonna della Misericordia*, located today in one of the rooms of Palazzo Salimbeni. The effort the bank

has put into the restoration and enhancement of the vast artistic heritage of the city and its province has contributed to making the representation of the artistic school of Siena ever more complete. Thus over the course of the last few decades an important collection of paintings, sculptures and furniture of the Sienese school from the 14th to the 19th century has been formed, one that can now stand alongside those of the city's more celebrated museums.

Or finally the patrimony of art of Intesa Sanpaolo, which represents the singular result of a diverse series of collecting choices, linked in an exemplary way to the history and tradition of the patronage of the different banks that make up the group. The cultural references illustrated by these collections of art are heterogeneous, embracing a very long span of time and the fruit of different aesthetic traditions while preserving, when considered individually, a strong cultural homogeneity and an ever higher and more widely recognized artistic quality.

A phenomenon, that of corporate collecting, which brings **eni** into line with the main Italian companies, but also with the American museum foundations, all born from private initiatives and whose patrimony comes not only from acquisitions but also from donations stemming from professional collaborations and the legacies of patrons and tycoons (for instance the works of Morandi, before being donated to the collection, were the personal property of Enrico Mattei).

Going rapidly into detail, we can say that the **eni** art collection represents some of the most significant moments in the history of art, in particular the second half of the 20th century, offering an important reflection on the forms that art has assumed over recent decades. The whole of the 20th century, in reality, was characterized by a climate of continual experimentation and the collection presents an unusual and evocative picture of that history, in the form of a dialogue between contrasting artistic languages that have found themselves in continual critical confrontation one with the other. A genuine anthology of the last century that takes us on a journey from the early avant-garde movements to the experiments of the postwar period.

Among the main subjects are still lifes, documented by the works of Giorgio Morandi (*Natura morta*, 1919), Filippo De Pisis (*Natura morta*, 1924) and Mario Mafai (*Natura morta con uova, pannocchie e gallo*, 1929). Then there are the elegant and enigmatic portraits of Felice Casorati; the naturalism *en plein air* of Arturo Tosi's landscapes; the simplification of color in the works of Fiorenzo Tomea; the stylistic synthesis of the image in Mario Sironi; the cubist decompositions of Renato Birolli (*Figura di donna*, 1947) and Bruno Cassinari, the solid realism of Renato Guttuso and Aligi Sassu (*Crocifissione*, 1953); and then from later years the transformation of the space and light in Enrico Castellani (*Superficie bianca*, 1980) and Alighiero Boetti (*Aeroplani*, 1990).

The collection also presents a cross-section of contemporary art with exponents of the caliber of Mimmo Rotella, Carla Accardi and Valerio Adami, who revisited the style of American pop art, developing it into a sort of fantastic and ironic comic strip. So from this perspective the **eni** collection represents a repository of different artistic languages that were continually influencing and holding a dialogue with one another, a place where art manifests itself as a kaleidoscope of color and light, a vivid testimony, in the moment of history in which we are living, to the way art aims to promote a dialogue beyond historical and cultural barriers.

The company's artistic heritage has been further enriched with a series of works by foreign artists who have maintained a constant and fertile dialogue with Italian artists. Among them Eugeniusz Eibisch, Polish painter, illustrator and educator, rector of Jagiellonian University in Kraków and a leading member of the Academy of Fine Arts in Warsaw; Salvatore Scarpitta (an Italian-American born in New York) who, while frequenting the principal American artists of the time, from Mark Rothko to David Smith, spent a lot of time in Italy where his friends included some of the painters most open to innovation and to the international scene (Burri, Dorazio, Fontana, Turcato, Consagra), an artist who in the sixties and seventies represented a current midway between Arte Povera and abstraction characterized by the technique of "bandaging," as his pictures were wrapped in webbing and canvas that were sometimes used to form the design, at others to block access to objects whose shape remained clearly visible (for example in the work *Face Trasp* of 1991, owned by **eni**); J.M. William Turner; Hussein el Gebali, one of the most important Egyptian lithographers who was born in Giza and graduated from the Faculty of Fine Arts of Cairo University but went on to study lithography at the Istituto di Belle Arti in Urbino; Ibrahim Kodra, whose light and unmistakable painting led Picasso, whom he knew and with whom he often worked in Italy, to declare that even his signature was a work of art. And then there is Hsiao Chin, a Chinese artist of exceptional talent whose creativity, rooted in Taoist practice and strengthened by his contacts with his Italian friends Fontana, Manzoni and Burri, led him to develop an absolutely new style of painting characterized by the juxtaposition of contrasting elements. Water-based paints are applied directly on canvas with tempera, India ink and colored inks without priming and on paper in an immediate and spontaneous manner in the attempt to capture simultaneously a sense of transcendence, tranquility, transparence, lucidity and illumination, enigmatic concepts that are typical and unanimously recognized elements of his art.

Another decidedly important part of the **eni** collection is made up of the large sculptures that ornament the offices in Milan and Rome. For example Floriano Boldini's *The Doves*, acquired out of a simple passion for beauty and art following the artist's solo exhibition at Gallarate in 1958. And then Francesco Messina, a favorite of a number of great poets who wrote about him (including Eugenio Montale) and a sculptor who received prestigious commissions from major collectors (for Giovanni Agnelli he made the statue of Saint Edward for the church of Sant'Edoardo in Sestriere).

The predilection for sculpture brought finally a series of great names like Aldo Caron (statue of Saint Barbara, 1957), a nonrepresentational artist who took his rejection of the figurative to its height in sculpture. Sculpture is by its nature material; three-dimensionality is its point of departure and arrival. To obey the same requirements of truth that have led to the accumulation of material in painting, sculpture took the opposite course: it destroyed its solidity in a process of erosion and annihilation.

This publication, as we have already stated, is born out of the desire to catalogue the **eni**'s artistic patrimony, offering an instrument of study as well as a contribution to making the history of the company more widely known through a collection that had never been catalogued before, and one which clearly demonstrates the passion for the history of art and culture that has characterized the company from the start. A cataloguing in which attention will be drawn not just to the more famous works but also to other less well-known ones that, within a process of development that is now evident, are no less significant.

CARLA ACCARDI

CARLA ACCARDI
Bianco - nero - corda, 1989

SERGIO ACCORSI
Pozzi Marini, n.d.

VALERIO ADAMI

VALERIO ADAMI
Tavola e città, 1991

ALI AL-ABANI
Raccolta dell'uva, n.d.

REMO ALDINI
Mareggiata, n.d.

ALIPIERI
Perforazioni petrolifere, 1962

B. ANDRÈS
Mercato indigeno nella foresta,
1962

STEFANO ARIENTI
Senza titolo, n.d.

A. ARTIOF
Astratto, n.d.

UGO ATTARDI
Tramonto e fiori, n.d.

SUSANA ATTIAS
Los gitanillos gipsy boys, 1986

MARCELLO AVENALI
Sogno di mille e una notte, n.d.

PIERRE BARAT
Paesaggio con lago, n.d.

PAOLO BARATTA
Autunno in tempo di guerra, 1919

SERGIO BARLETTA
Accampamento, n.d.

ERALDO BIGARELLI
Omaggio all'Agip, 1988

ERALDO BIGARELLI
Paesaggio con alberi, 1990

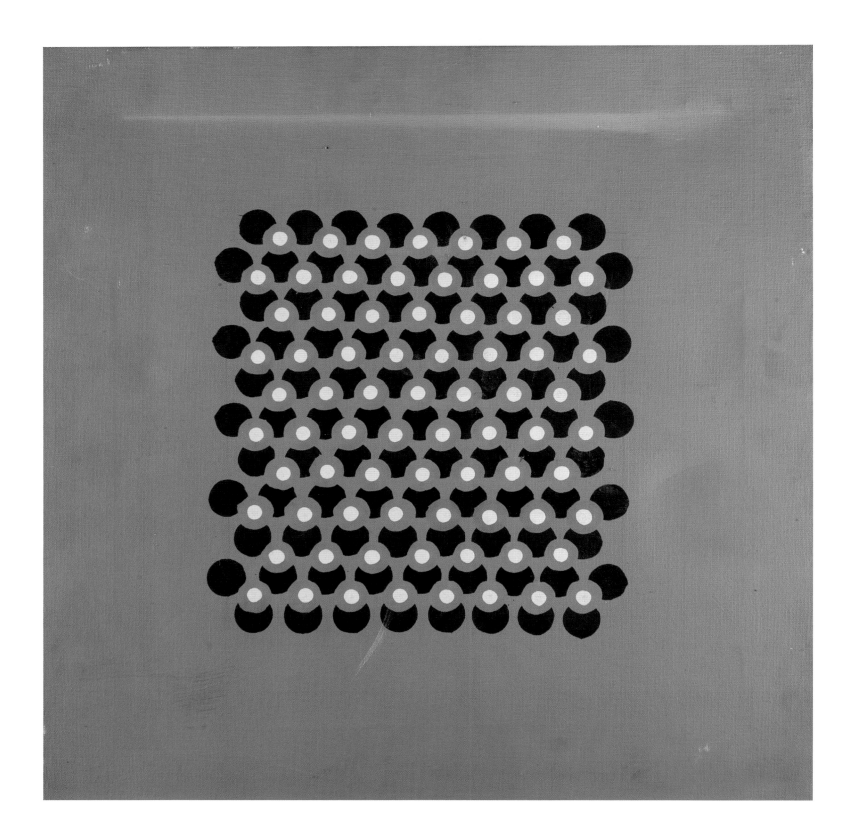

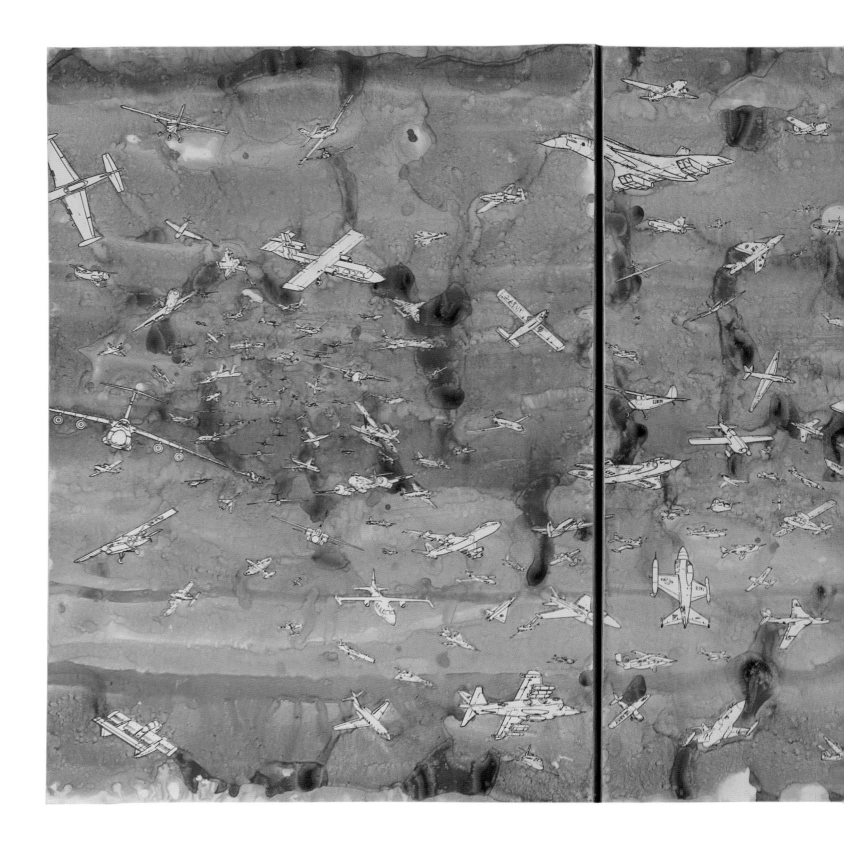

ALIGHIERO BOETTI
Aeroplani, 1990

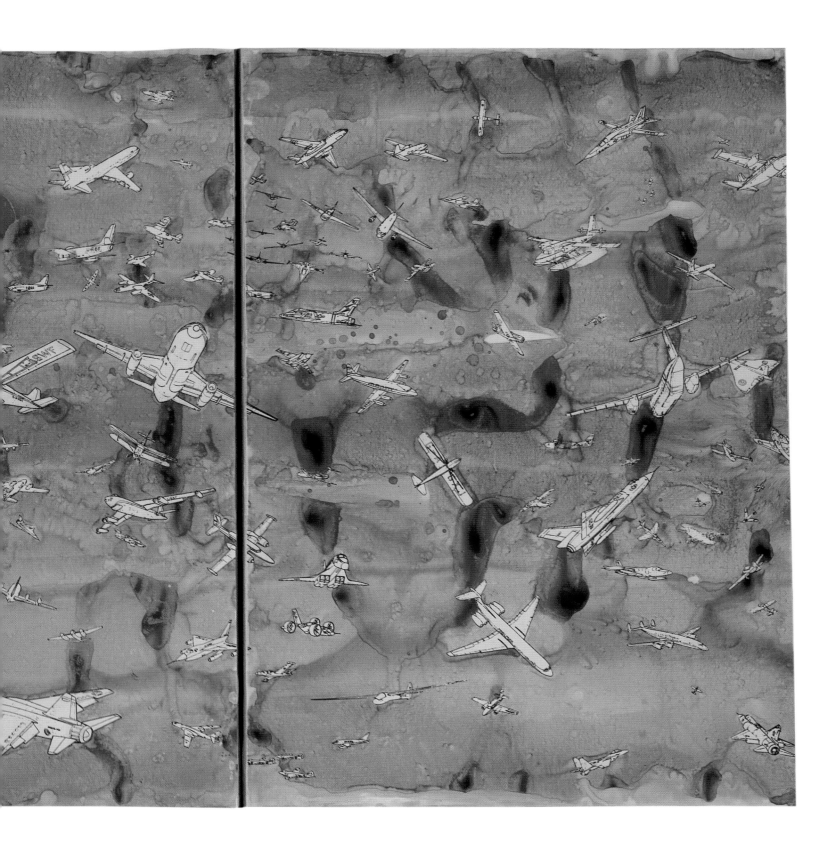

LUIGI BOILLE
Al Raimy, Al Khayt, 1979

FRANZ BORGHESE
Personaggi, n.d.

DINO BOSCHI
Motore città, 1970

CESARE BREVEGLIERI
Cortiletto, n.d.

CESARE BREVEGLIERI
Chiesetta, n.d.

ANTONIO BUENO
Figura in rosa, 1970

UMBERTO BUSCIONI
Un mare di cravatte, 1969

UMBERTO BUSCIONI
Particolari, 1969

VINCENZO CAMERLINGO
Carrozze nel viale, 1942

VINCENZO CAMERLINGO
Mercato, 1942

VINCENZO CAMERLINGO
Veduta di canale, 1942

VINCENZO CAMERLINGO
Veduta di porto, 1942

DOMENICO CANTATORE
Natura morta, 1959

DOMENICO CANTATORE
Natura morta di oggetti /
Oggetti sul tavolo, 1960

GIOVANNI CAPPELLI
Raffineria di notte, 1980

LUIGI CARBONI
Senza titolo, 1990

ALDO CARON
Evolvente n. 2, 1984

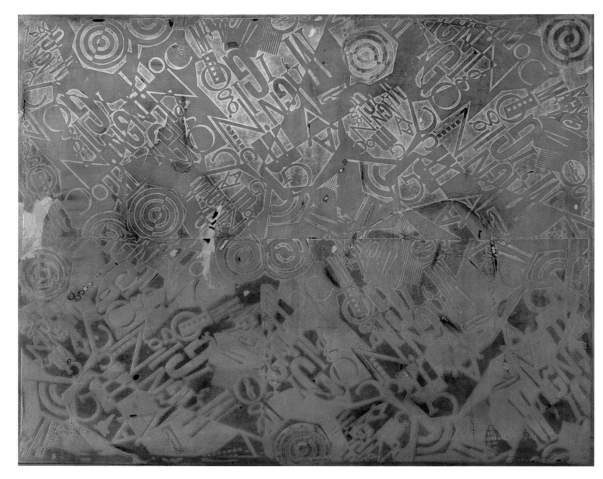

MICHELE CASCELLA
Paesaggio invernale, n.d.

MICHELE CASCELLA
Campo di carciofi, n.d.

FELICE CASORATI
Ritratto di signora, n.d.

UMBERTO CASOTTI
Astratto, 1965

BRUNO CASSINARI
Natura morta, 1968

BRUNO CASSINARI
Madonna con Bambino, n.d.

BRUNO CASSINARI
Ritratto antico, n.d.

ENRICO CASTELLANI

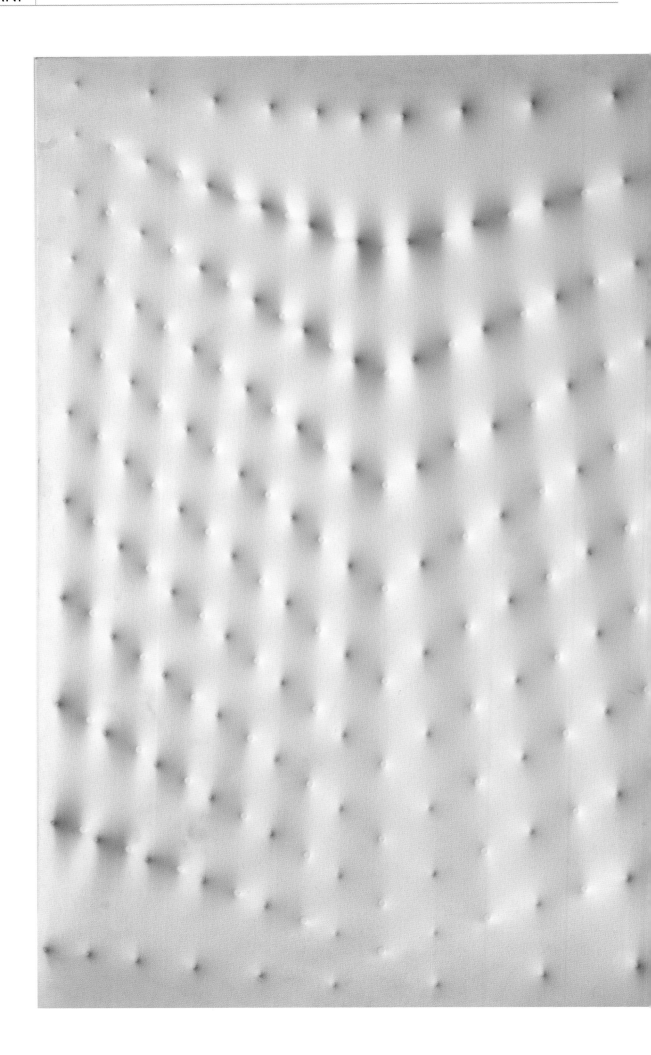

ENRICO CASTELLANI
Superficie bianca, 1980

CAVEDON
Porto industriale, n.d.

GIUSEPPE CESETTI
Cavalli maremmani, n.d.

ALFREDO CHIGHINE
Natura morta con chitarra, 1949

ALFREDO CHIGHINE
Paesaggio A1, 1952

HSIAO CHIN
Figura astratta, n.d.

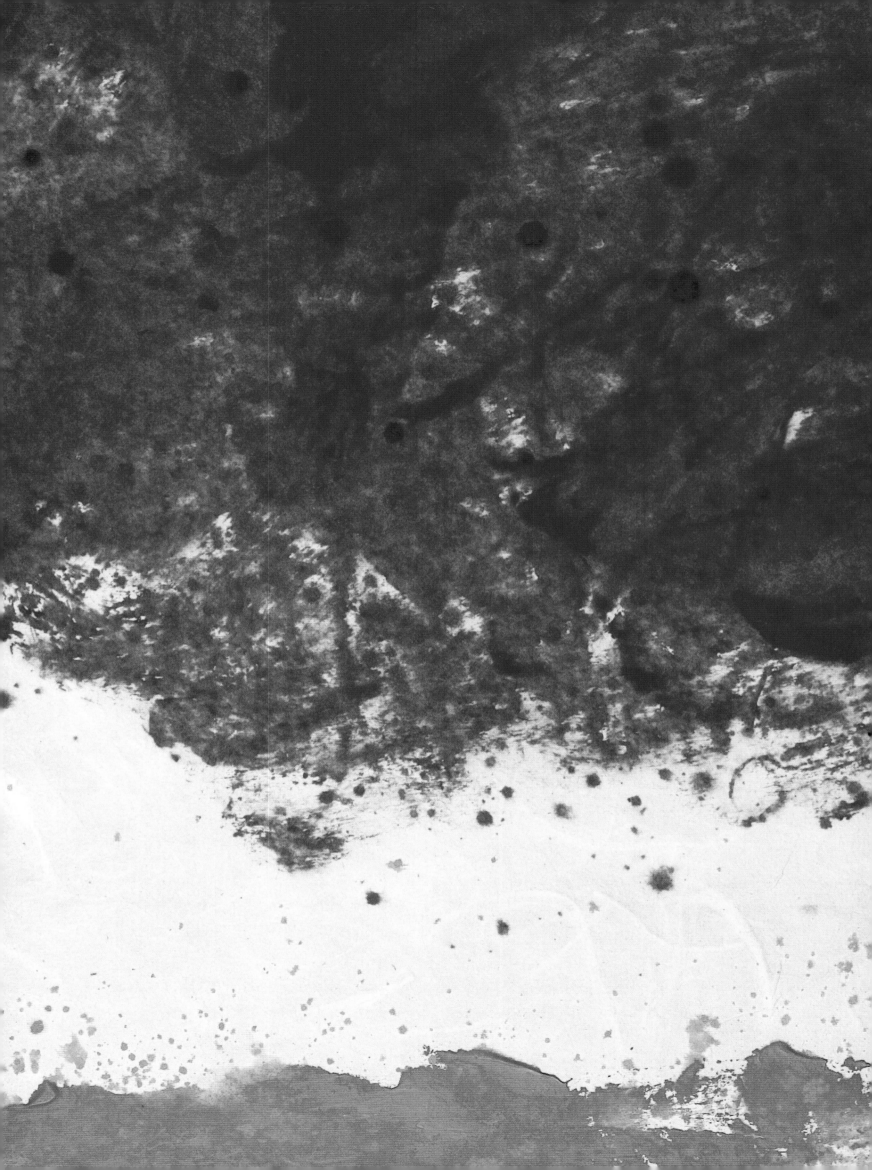

VALENTINO CIUSANI
Corpo leggero, 1990

VALENTINO CIUSANI
In verde età, 1991

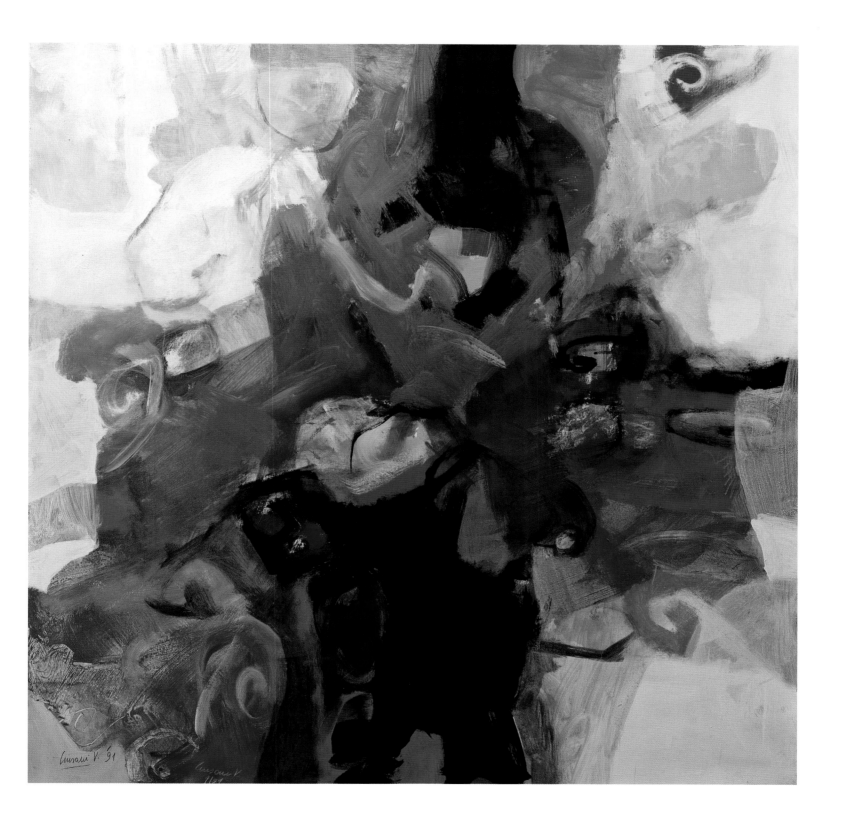

RUDOLF CLAUDUS
*Torpediniera Calatafimi (attacco
di Genova 1940)*, 1951

FABRIZIO CLERICI
Deserto, n.d.

GIUSEPPE COMINETTI
Maratoneti (figure di sportivi),
n.d.

J. DEAN
Color hearts, 1970

DON UGO DE CENSI
Sostando in un prato, n.d.

FILIPPO DE PISIS
Natura morta, 1924

LUCIANO DE VITA
Marina, n.d.

ANGELO DEL BON
Adda a Airuno, n.d.

ANGELO DEL BON
Città, n.d.

U. DEL CORNO
Fiume e barche sulla riva, 1955

MARIO DELUIGI
GVJ50 "Grattage", 1966

**GIUSEPPE SEBASTIANO
DEVOTI**
*Due edifici in mezzo al mare
e cielo verde*, n.d.

**GIUSEPPE SEBASTIANO
DEVOTI**
*Due edifici in mezzo a un prato
e cielo arancione*, n.d.

AMA DI IBRA
Città e Campagna, n.d.

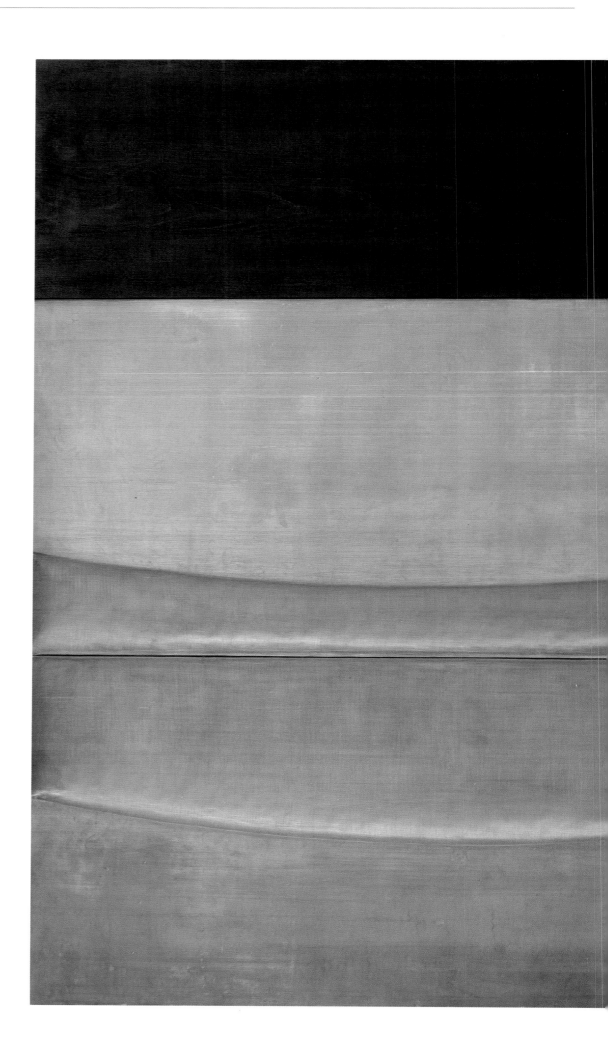

NUNZIO DI STEFANO
Niger, 1990

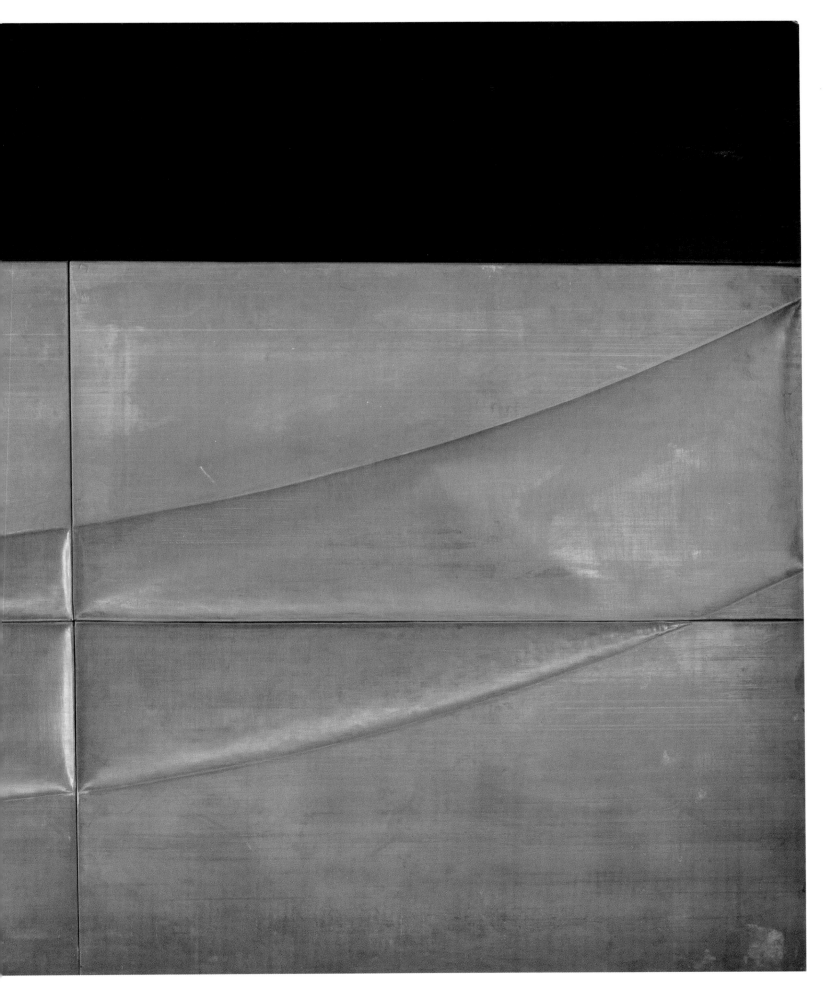

PIETRO DODERO
Madre e figlio con natura morta,
1978

DOMMIMI
Maschera di ferro, n.d.

D. CHESS DOUGLAS
Deli - personaggi *per strada*,
1987

D. CHESS DOUGLAS
Carrarmato, 1987

EUGENIUSZ EIBISCH
Fagiano, 1967

ENZO FARAONI
Figura di donna, 1973

FERNANDO FARULLI
Stabilimento, 1958

FERNANDO FARULLI
Stabilimento, 1959

FERNANDO FARULLI
Il sonno, 1962

SALVATORE FIUME

SALVATORE FIUME
Figura femminile, 1980

**GUSTAVO FRANCALANCIA
DI RICCARDO**
Deserto libico, 1980

CESARE GALOFARO
Distributore sotto la pioggia,
1945

MARCOLINO GANDINI
Arabeschi, 1979

ALBERTO GARUTTI
Senza titolo, 1991

Prova d'artista   al sig Cefis
                                   cordialmente Gentilini

FRANCO GENTILINI
Vasi e fiori, n.d.

PIERO GILARDI
Tronchi di pino, 1990

GUSTAVO GIULIETTI
La castità, 1970

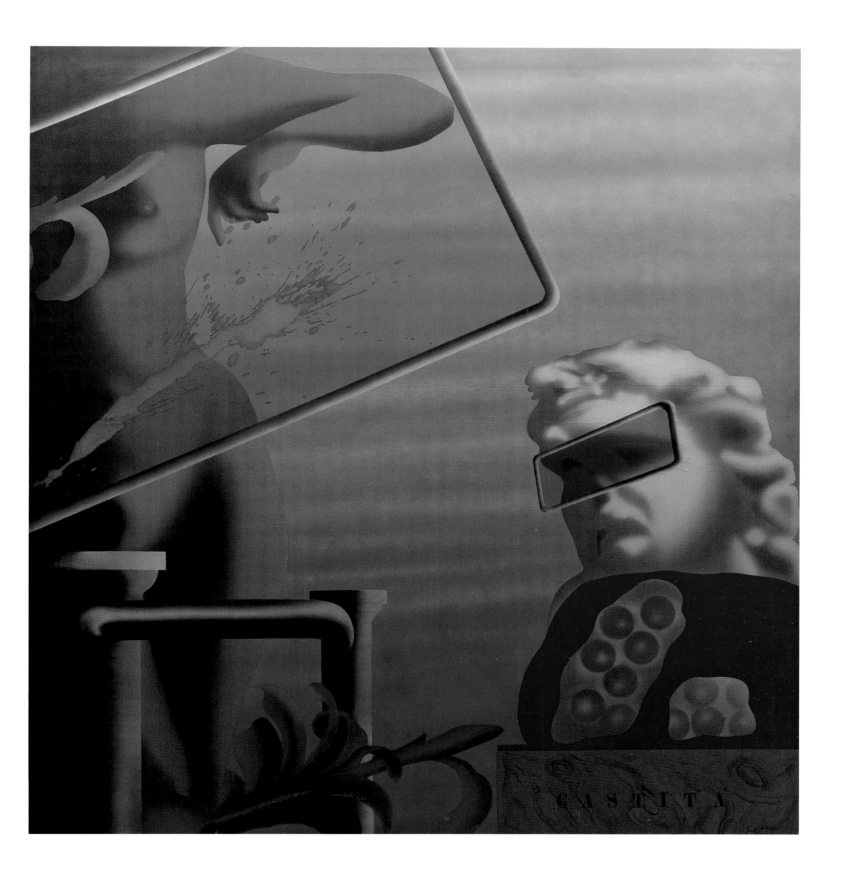

MARCEL GOTÈNE
Soggetto astratto, 1993

MARCEL GOTÈNE
Soggetto astratto, 1993

MARCEL GOTÈNE
Il mercato, 1995

MARCEL GOTÈNE
La pesca, 1995

GIUSEPPE GUIDOTTI
Carnevale, 1971

GIUSEPPE GUIDOTTI
Embrione in formazione, 1972

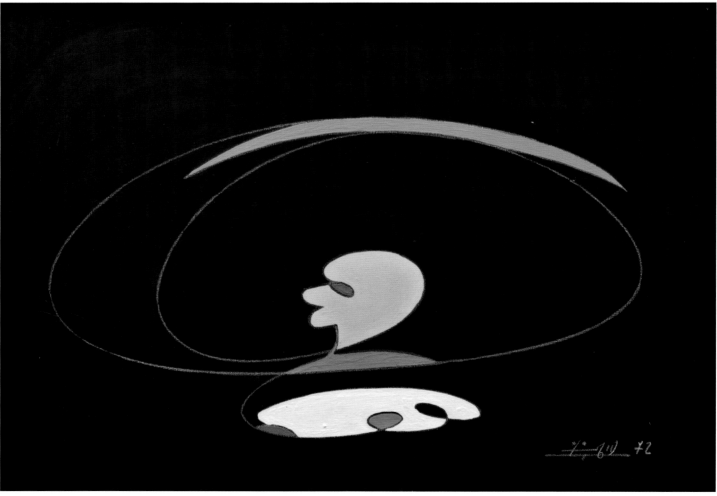

J. GULCI
Bosco invernale, n.d.

RENATO GUTTUSO

RENATO GUTTUSO
Paesaggio predesertico,
1978 circa

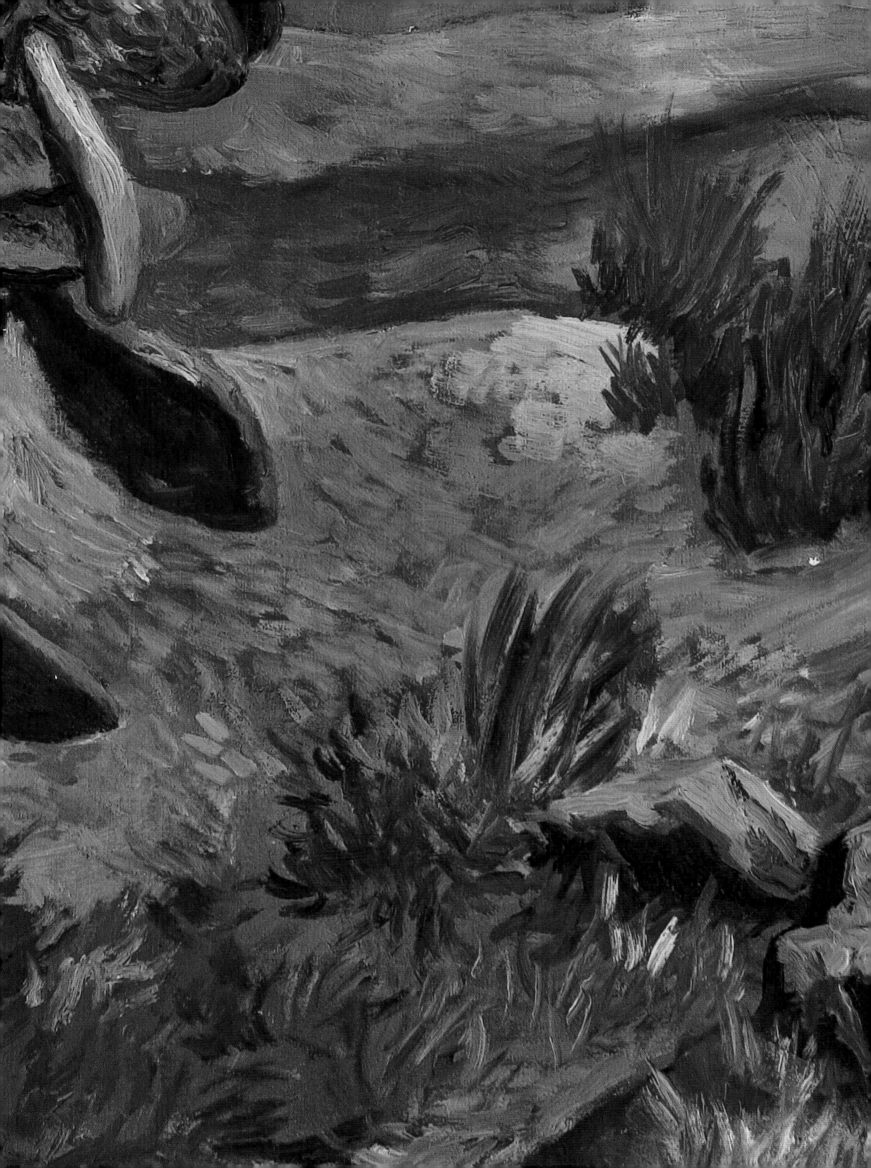

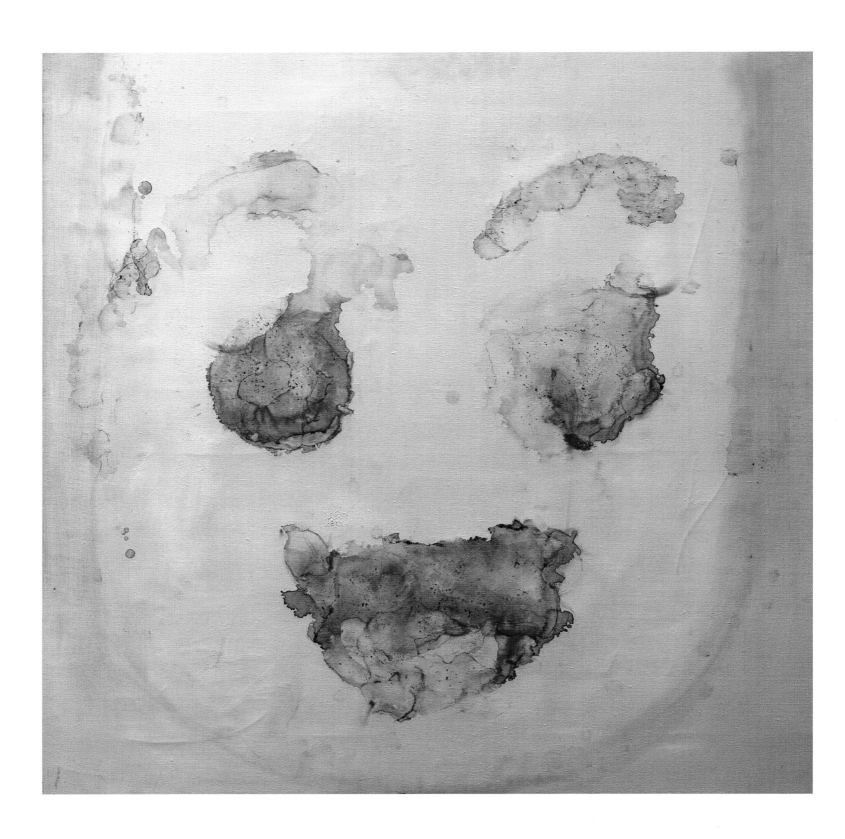

IBRAHIM KODRA
Sul fiume verde, n.d.

LITZ
Senza titolo, n.d.

MARIO MAFAI
Natura morta con uova,
pannocchie e gallo, 1929

159

EGISTO MAGNI
Senza titolo, n.d.

EGISTO MAGNI
Senza titolo, n.d.

EGISTO MAGNI
Senza titolo, n.d.

EGISTO MAGNI
Senza titolo, n.d.

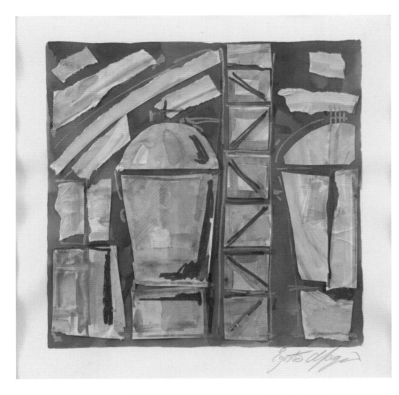

FEDERICO MARAGLIANO
Sole e ombra, n.d.

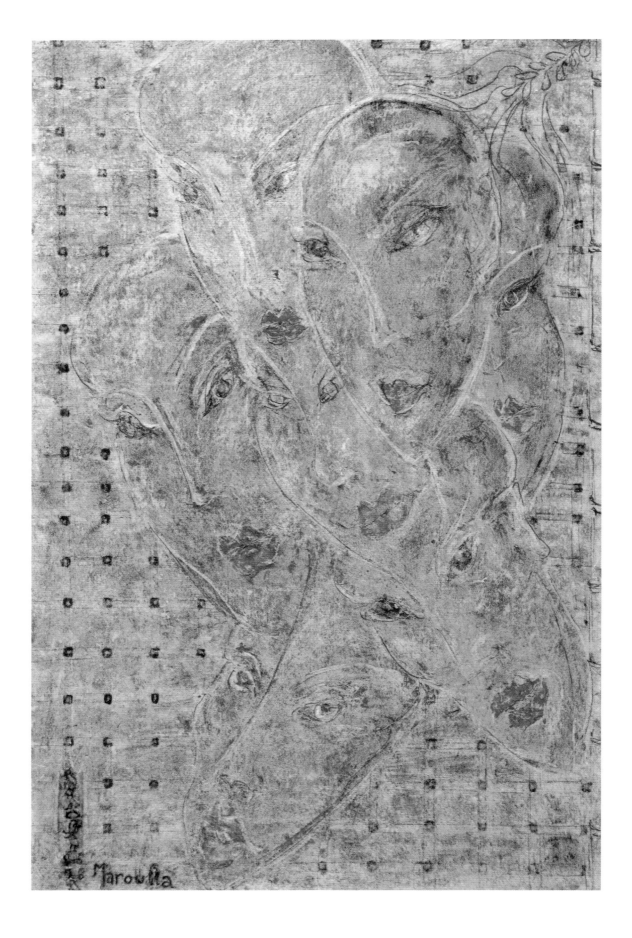

GIUSEPPE MEGNA
Minareti, 1980

FRANCO MIELE
Campagna meridionale, 1952

MILANI
Senza titolo, n.d.

MILANI
Senza titolo, n.d.

GIORGIO MORANDI
Natura morta, 1919

GIORGIO MORANDI
Natura morta, 1941

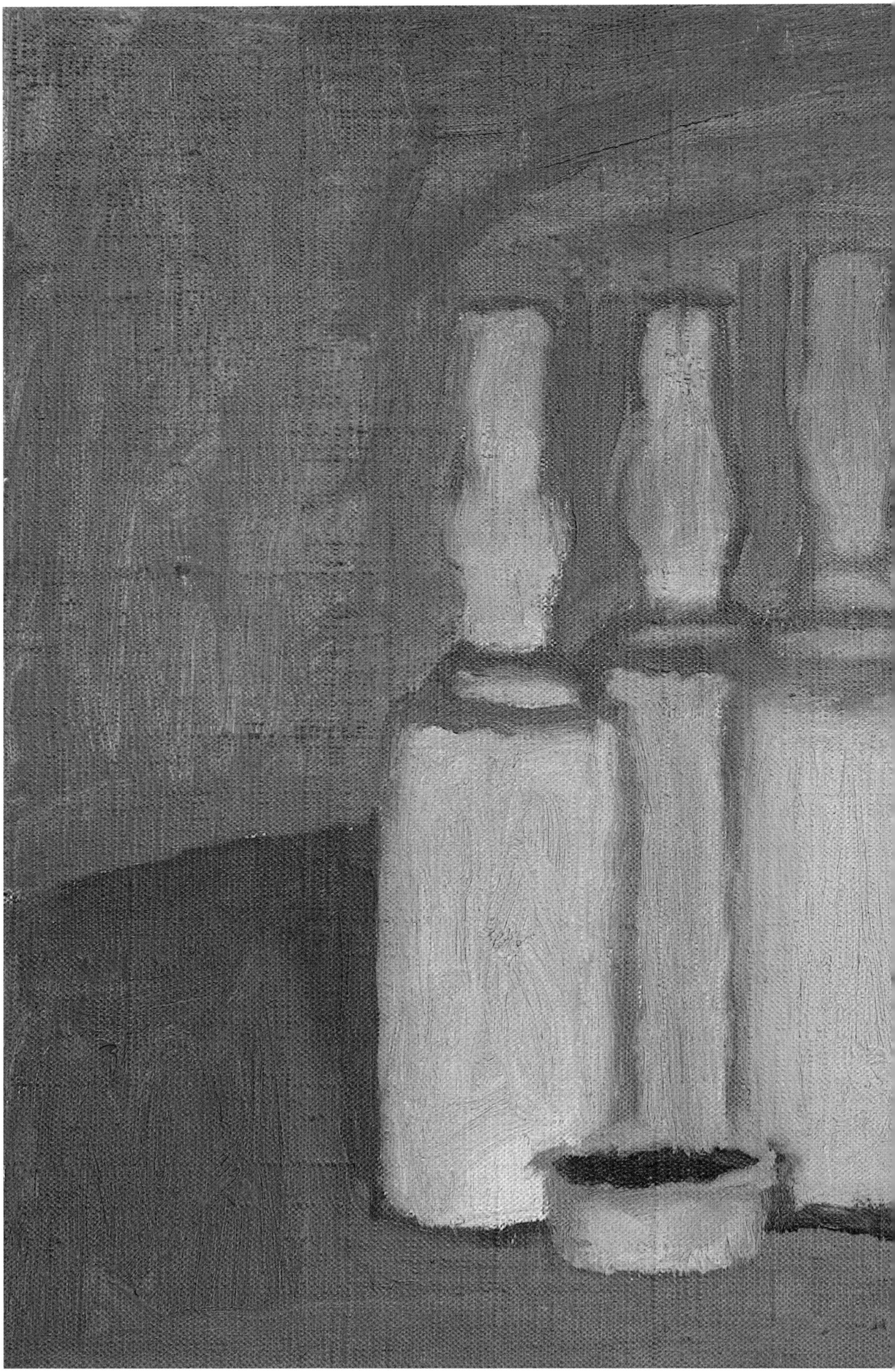

ANTONIO TONO MUCCHI
La villa, 1981

ANTONIO TONO MUCCHI
Due luci nel crepuscolo, 1988

GIULIA NAPOLEONE
Rifrazioni, 1980

VITTORIO NATTINO
Prato Fiorito, n.d.

LUCIANA NOTTURNI
Piattaforma, n.d.

R. NOVELLI
Fabbriche e case (cantiere),
1991

ODIM
Astratto rosso e bianco materico,
1963

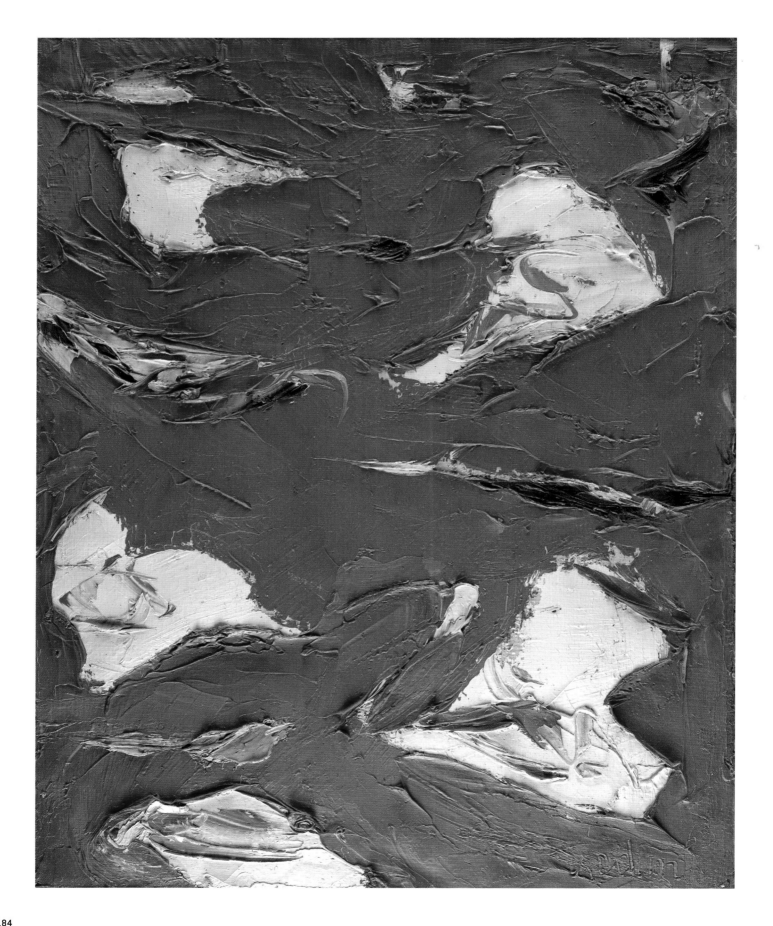

S. KRISTEN OHEN
Senza titolo, n.d.

LUIGI ONTANI
Il giglio di Virgilio, 2006

GIUSEPPE PENNASILICO

GIUSEPPE PENNASILICO
*Lavoratori all'Argano (bozzetto
del grande dipinto)*, 1920

GIUSEPPE PENNASILICO
*Lavoratori all'Argano (cantiere
navale)*, 1920

ALFONSO PONE
Paesaggio Dorato, 1958

UMBERTO POSTAL
Omologazioni, 1992/1993
with fluorescent lightbox on and off

MARIO PUCCIARELLI
Comparizione, 1966

ENOTRIO PUGLIESE
La torre di Briatico, n.d.

ENOTRIO PUGLIESE
Torre Normanna, n.d.

ENOTRIO PUGLIESE
Casello ferroviario, circa 1960

G. RAB
Composizione, n.d.

S. RICCIARDELLI
Senza titolo, n.d.

FABIO RIETI
Le amiche, 1970

FABIO RIETI
Grattacieli, 1997

FABIO RIETI
Grattacieli e case dall'alto,
1997

FABIO RIETI
Ragazzo seduto affacciato
alla finestra sulla città,
1997

OTTONE ROSAI
Strada, casa e un albero, 1935

OTTONE ROSAI
Paesaggio, 1947

MIMMO ROTELLA
Un momento trasversale, 1990

ANTONIO SALIOLA
Le linee del cielo, 1980

ALBERTO SARTORIS
Composizione, 1965

ALIGI SASSU
Crocifissione, 1953

RUGGERO SAVINIO
La conversazione di Cetona,
1990

MARIO SCHINAIA
Omaggio a Calderon de la barca,
1984

MARIO SCHINAIA
Specchi in vetro, n.d.

MARIO SCHINAIA
Mare barocco n. 2, 1984

MARIO SCHINAIA
Hypons n. 2, 1985

TOTI SCIALOJA
Composizione, 1980

MARIO SIRONI

MARIO SIRONI
Composizione sacra, 1922

MARIO SIRONI
Cantiere, n.d.

MARIO SIRONI
Composizione, 1947

MARIO SIRONI
Due figure, 1950

GIULIO SORDINI
Rondini, 1959

ADRIANO SPILIMBERGO
Veduta di Milano, circa 1950

SPINETI
Senza titolo, 1983

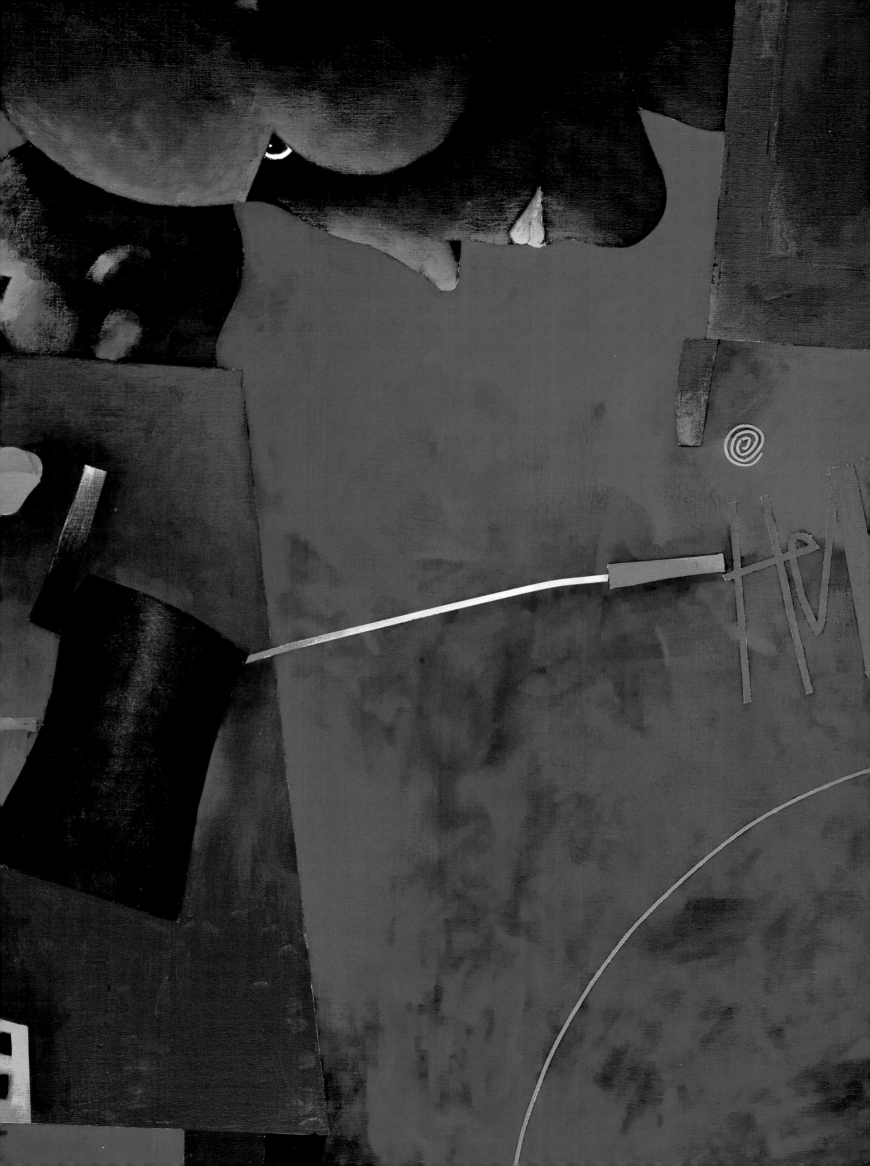

SERENA TALLARIGO
Composition, 1983

SERENA TALLARIGO
Composizione, 1987

SERENA TALLARIGO
Composizione, 1987

ORFEO TAMBURI
Quai de la Seine, n.d.

ORFEO TAMBURI
Quai de la Seine, n.d.

ORFEO TAMBURI
Ritratto di Blaise Cendrars, 1949

MARIO TARCHETTI
Barche in costruzione, n.d.

FIORENZO TOMEA
Autunno a Zoppè, 1941

FIORENZO TOMEA
*Paesaggio (Case di Zoppè
di Cadore)*, 1954

FIORENZO TOMEA
Case di sera a Zoppè, 1955

EUGENIO TOMIOLO
Senza titolo, 1940

ARTURO TOSI
Ulivi del Garda, 1933

ARTURO TOSI
Paesaggio, 1935

ARTURO TOSI
Paesaggio, circa 1940

ARTURO TOSI
Paesaggio della Val Seriana,
circa 1940

ARTURO TOSI
Paesaggio, n.d.

ARTURO TOSI
Paesaggio, n.d.

ANTONIO TOTERO
Fantasia Medio Orientale, n.d.

FERNANDO TROSO
Pastorello in un paesaggio, 1972

ALDO TURCHIARO
Barca all'orizzonte, 1980

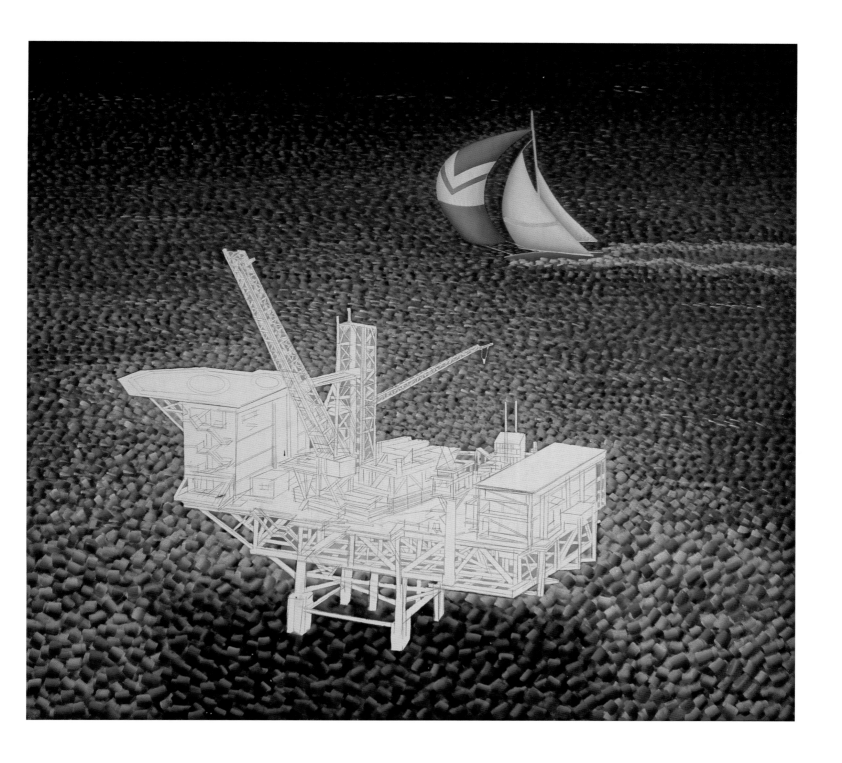

ANTONIO VANGELLI
Cavalli e clowns, 1960

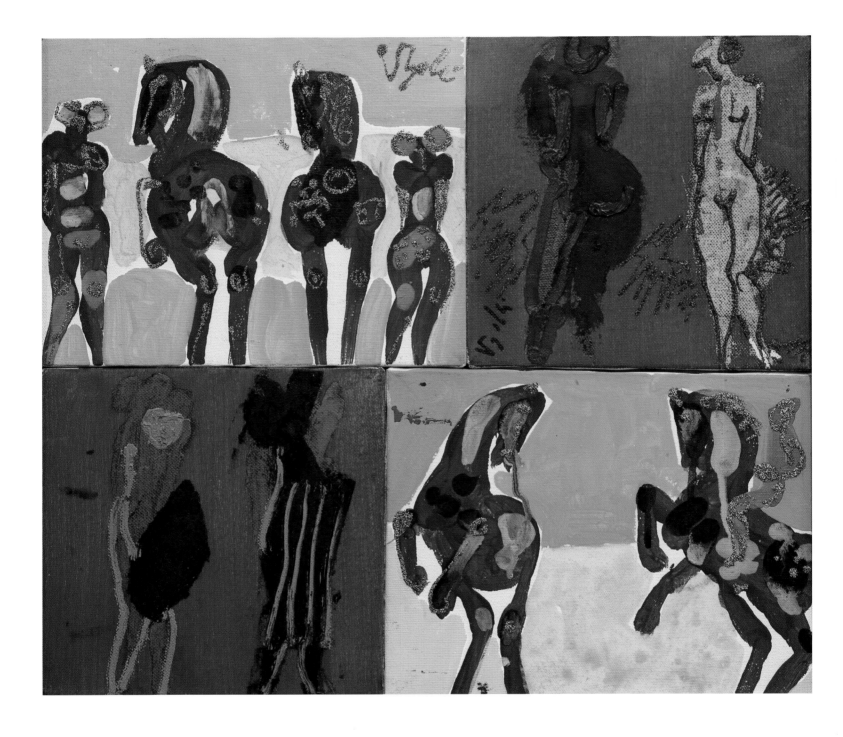

ANTONIO VANGELLI
Giocolieri del circo, 1960

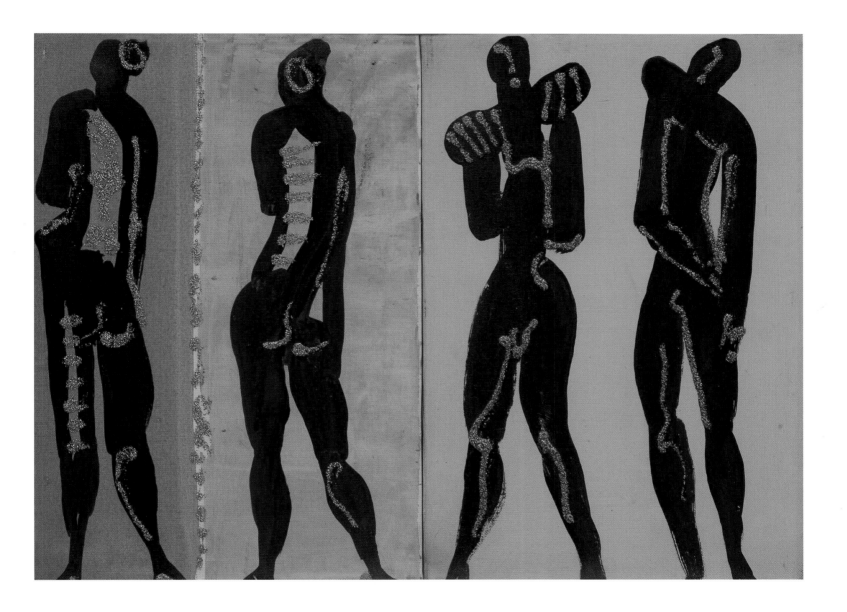

MARIO VELLANI MARCHI
Giovani merlettaie, 1952

RENZO VESPIGNANI
Stabilimento petrolchimico, 1955

RENZO VESPIGNANI
Ritratto di Nietta, 1970

MANDY WILKINSON
Senza titolo, n.d.

GEIRA AUESTAD WOITIER
Fiori, n.d.

YVAN
Astratto, 1970

CESARE ZAMPALONI
Roma-periferia, n.d.

EMNA ZGHAL
L'eccellenza tecnologica, 1995

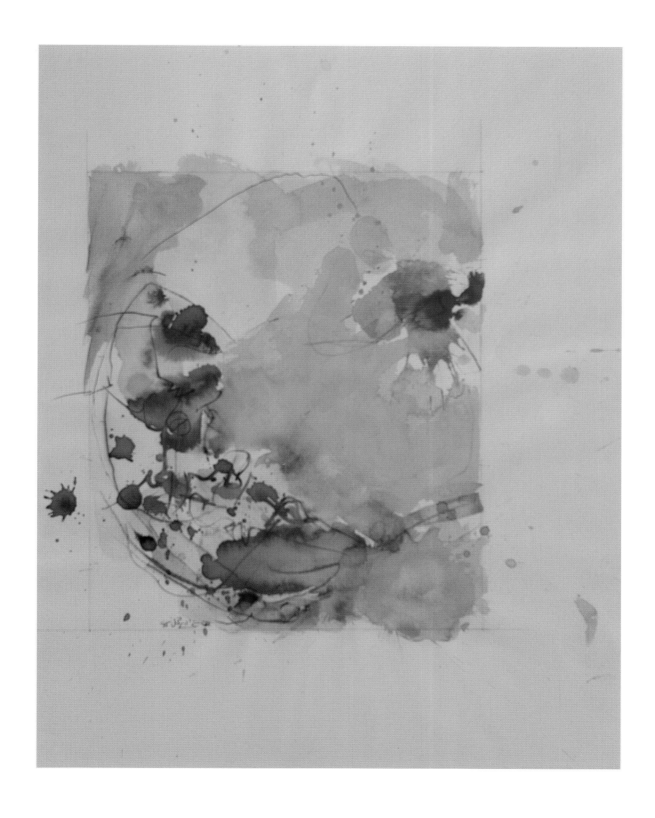

the fondo folon

Cinzia Chiari
*Responsible for the cataloguing of **eni**'s art collections*

the world of jean-michel folon

I think that art is like bread and water: you cannot do without it,
you need to have a daily ration of it to live.
That's how I feel and how I am. I need to discover something every day,
otherwise I'm unhappy. I need this sense of wonder.
J.M.F.

Jean-Michel Folon was a leading figure on the international art scene, known above all for the poetic world that peopled his watercolors. His career was a poetic and visual journey of profound originality.

Born in a suburb of Brussels in 1934, Folon gave up his studies of architecture to move to Paris in 1955. After trying in vain to get his drawings published, he decided to send them, in 1960, to some of the most prestigious magazines in America, including *The New Yorker*, which published them immediately. So Folon began his creative journey as a draftsman and illustrator, an activity that he was never to abandon. After a period in the United States, he returned to Paris in 1964 and showed his works there, designing for the promotion of the exhibition the first in a long series of posters that were to characterize his production right up until his death, in Montecarlo in October 2005.

From the second half of the sixties and over the following decades, Folon also devoted himself to the illustration of books, from Giorgio Soavi's *Le message* to French editions of Borges's *The Circular Ruins* and Kafka's *Metamorphosis* and the complete works of Jacques Prévert. In the eighties he started to design scenery for numerous musical and theatrical works, from Puccini to Stravinsky's *Histoire du soldat* and the plays of Carlo Goldoni. At the same time, he produced a series of cartoons for tapestries made by the Aubusson Factory and for a large mosaic. Two retrospective exhibitions held in Japan and at the Museo Correr in Venice in 1985 set the seal on Folon's worldwide reputation.

Over the course of the eighties the artist also began to carve small wooden sculptures, which would be shown at the Metropolitan Museum of Art in New York in 1990, along with watercolors, engravings and recycled and transformed objects. Finally, in the nineties, Folon tackled sculpture in bronze: some pieces of a large size can be seen in Paris, Barcelona, Marseilles and Brussels. One of most beautiful is the bronze *L'Inconnu* ("The Unknown," 1993), owned by **eni**.

What makes Folon's sculpture fascinating is the apparent contrast between the impalpable lightness of the images that emanates from the watercolors, an evanescent world of pale and mellow colors, and the dense materiality of the bronze with which the artist expressed himself in his last years (as well as with terracotta, another extremely concrete and opaque material). And yet there is an inner consistency, a mysterious continuum between two such different, almost antithetical techniques, as a result of which the bronze with its patina seems to be magically set free of its weight.

The absolute protagonist of his watercolors and plastic works is the "little man," the *Quelqu'un* with an almost featureless face and tall hat, often represented holding a suitcase or a book, in a sort of eternal suspension between the mental, and wholly inner, journey of reading and the impossible physical journey, evoked by the raimbow-shaped baggage of *Uomo con arcobaleno* (1998), or the one with a ship looming on the horizon in *Senza titolo* (watercolor on paper, 1998). The journey, in fact, is always a departure "for the unknown lands of inner distance," as the artist put it.

Linked to this idea of the voyage or journey, the ship is another mythical symbol that plays a leading role in Folon's imagery, and can be found in the watercolors and the object-sculptures he created out of a variety of salvaged materials, as in *E la nave va*, realized in 1992 out of wood and cast iron, with its intentional reference to the title of the movie made by his friend Fellini. Federico Fellini, an admirer of Folon's work, met him on the set of *Casanova* and formed a fruitful relationship of friendship and collaboration with him. Later Fellini would recall: "I believe in light, and light has to be what the imagination demands. Folon's light will never be the one that the sun can give. He has invented a strange light, coming from somewhere else ... I too invent the cinema which I need ... I reconstructed the sea in *Amarcord*. And nothing is truer than that sea on the screen ... Folon has reconstructed imaginary blue cities. And nothing is truer than those cities on paper."

And in fact Folon reworked all the past in a fabulous and magical dimension, as has rightly been pointed out by another great artist, Emilio Tadini, whose work presents many affinities with that of the Belgian painter: "A work by Folon brings us close to the world of fable. So close that at times it seems to be on the point of transferring us, bag and baggage, into that open, gaping, free dimension."

eni possesses hundreds of Folon's works, fruit of an artistic association that linked him for many years to Italgas. From 1991 onward Folon and SNAM collaborated on advertising campaigns that set out to illustrate the environmentally friendly characteristics of methane in a calm and simple tone, chiefly through the use of the language of poetry. One of these campaigns, which had a powerful impact and has remained in the collective imagination, was centered on an animated film lasting sixty seconds, made jointly by SNAM and the Distributors's Associations. Through Folon's highly distinctive style—his mechanized and uniform universe, inhabited by delicately bewildered men and characterized by a masterly use of watercolor and a meticulous allusive precision—SNAM wanted to communicate the importance of methane in the landscape of daily life: methane as a source of energy that respected the environment. The spot was accompanied by murals, communication events and cultural and artistic initiatives that contributed to the success of methane in Italy. In his colorful, reflective and dreamy style, fantastic and yet simple, the artist would go on to represent in various ways the lightness of natural gas, its environmental advantages and, at the same time, the long journey that it had to make to reach our homes from distant gas fields, crossing deserts, seas and mountains.

In demonstration of the artistic value of this collaboration, the video of the SNAM advertising campaign is on show in a dedicated space with a fairytale atmosphere (a room completely lined with mirrors) at the Fondation Folon. The foundation was opened by the artist himself on October 27, 2000, in the park of La Hulpe in the environs of Brussels, and now displays over three hundred of his works. A museum that presents more than forty years of the artist's activity, in a lively and original setting.

In fact what Jean-Michel Folon opened was the book of his own life (the entrance is in the shape of a large book of fairytales that opens every 20 seconds) and page after page the visitor discovers the different aspects of his art and his world: watercolors, silkscreen prints, engravings, posters, objects, stained glass, sculptures, music, films and optical effects animate an interactive route, studied for his public. The original circuit, designed by Folon for the foundation, has in fact interactive sections and takes the viewer on a poetic and dreamy journey into the heart of his creation, culminating in the fantastic projection room, where the video of the SNAM advertising campaign represents perfectly the commitment of **eni** and Folon to one of the most important issues in the world: that of the environment, of how technology can coexist with nature, and of how it is often possible for technology and energy to safeguard that environment.

In demonstration of that shared commitment, the company houses in its collection an even greater number of watercolors than the Fondation Folon itself, a deposit that is the fruit of an intuition on the part of the **eni** executives, who have always made use of art in their communications on the subject of energy, as if art and energy were two aspects of one and the same thing.

And in fact when Folon passed away Italgas staged an open-air exhibition at its headquarters in Turin: twenty-six of the Belgian artist's works were projected onto the façades of the building in a homage to the artist who was for Italgas the mind and the heart of one of the most important advertising campaigns ever produced, and one that made Folon's name known even to members of the public who knew little about art. The pastel images with the little flame that illustrated the SNAM campaign and the slogan "methane gives you a hand" have gone down in the history of advertising. It was for this reason that Italgas, paying tribute to the artist who best represented its brand, sponsored the major anthological exhibition of 250 works, "Folon-Firenze," held in the spaces of the Forte di Belvedere and the Sala d'Arme in Palazzo Vecchio in Florence in May 2005.

In addition to advertising, however, Folon never relinquished the social and civil commitment that led him to work with Amnesty International, putting his creativity at the service of the defense of human rights, and for this he was made an ambassador of UNICEF.

And so the decision to devote one section of its collection to Folon's genius is not just a recognition of the artist's contribution to its advertising, but also of the way that he shared the values of a great company, whose growth has never been at the expense of the rights of weaker members of society or the protection of the environment.

Regarded as a "philosopher of the marvelous," a multifaceted artist who produced watercolors, etchings, engravings, sculptures, posters, murals, stained glass and photographs, without forgetting theatrical scenery and book illustrations, of great evocative power and expressive and poetic intensity, Folon therefore bears ideal witness to that relationship between art, environment and enterprise which is now considered essential and indispensable by so much of contemporary culture and which has always been at the base of **eni**'s engagement in the world.

Autunno, 1995

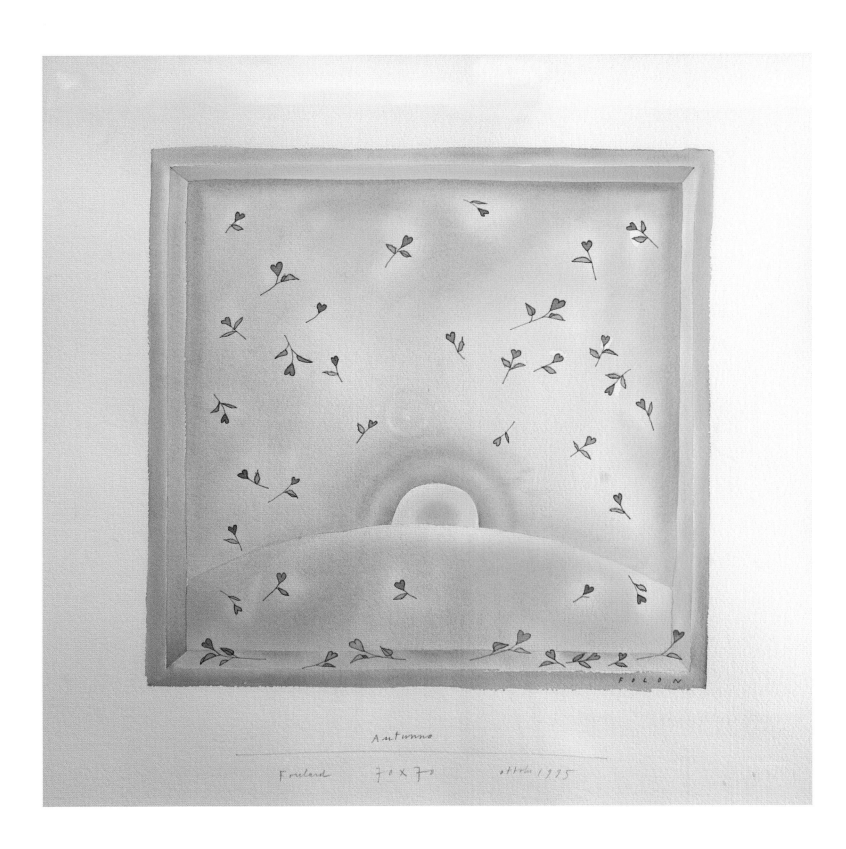

Lucido per la Fenice, 1995

Sketches (no. 4 panels), n.d.

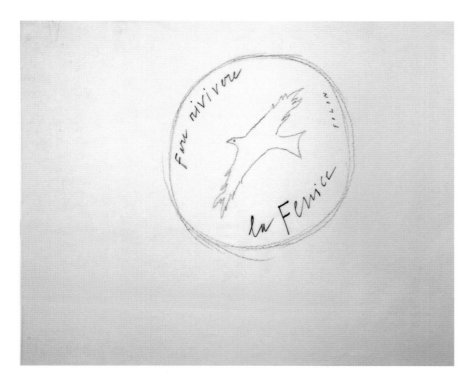

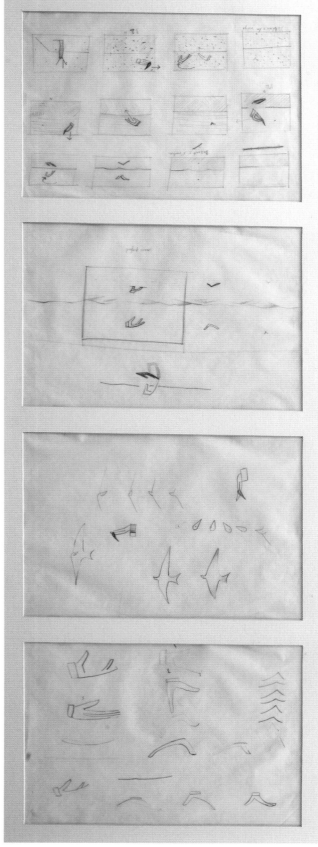

Testa di gabbiano, 1995

Finestra aperta, 1997

*Testa di gabbiano-con dedica
alla Snam*, 1995

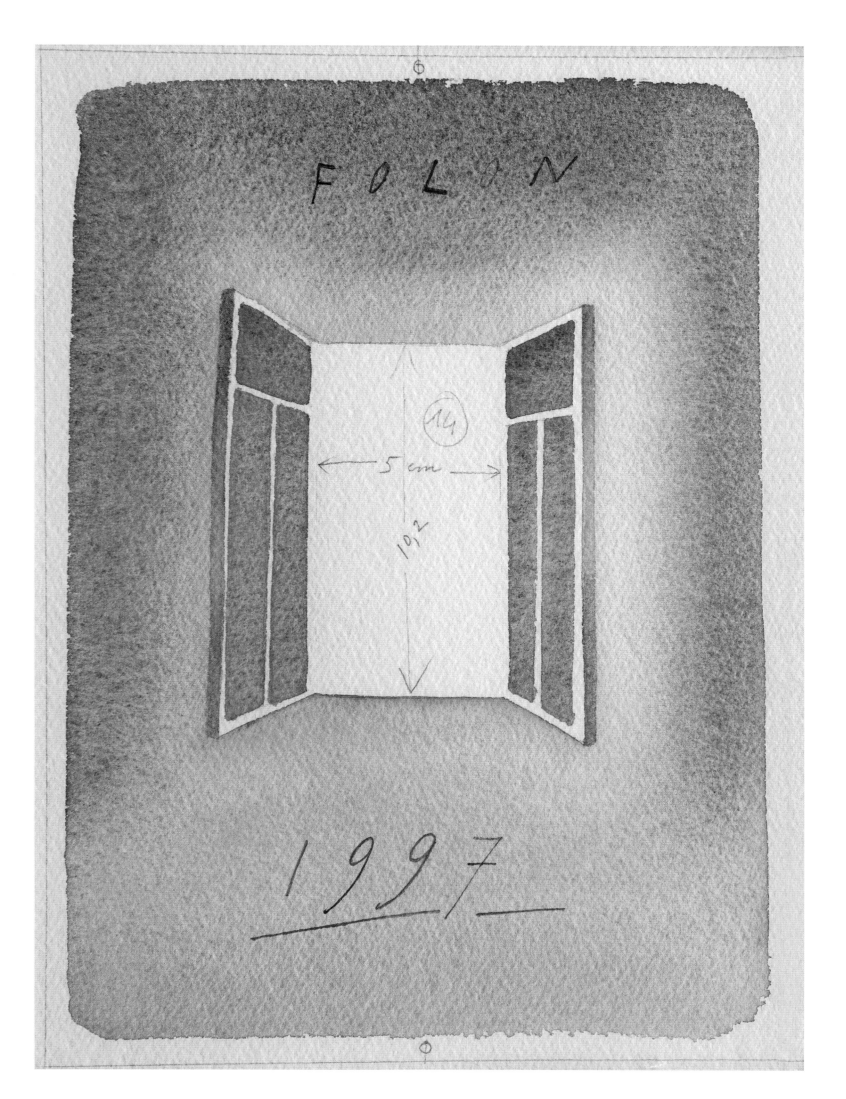

FOLON

14

5 cm

10,2

1997

Uomo con fuoco in mano,
1997

S in cielo, n.d.

Proposta logo EUROGAS, n.d.

Le gaz naturel, il calore
di ogni giorno, n.d.

Proposta logo EUROGAS
albero con fiammelle blu, n.d.

Le gas naturel   Il calore di ogni giorno

J 14 Mai

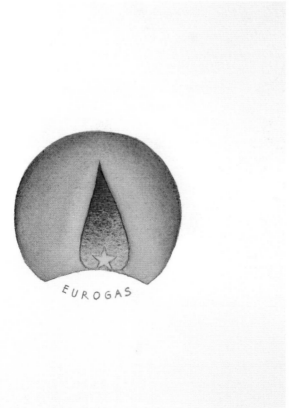

EUROGAS

EUROGAS

Keith Jarrett, 1998

Autobus blu, 1998

Multipla dietro, n.d.

Multipla lato destro, n.d.

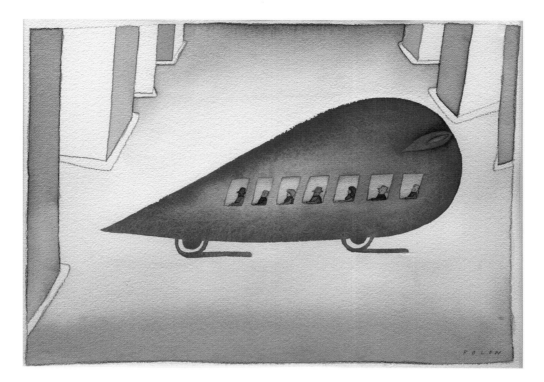

*Pesciolino nella bottiglia
(piccola)*, 1998

Il metano viene dalla natura,
1998

Mani con fiammelle, 1998

Un uomo che scende da un
cielo proiettato, 1998

Uomo che esce dal cielo
(campagna), 1998

*Uomo che esce dal cielo
(campagna)*, 1998

Uomo con arcobaleno, 1998   *Uomo con valigia*, 1998

Uomo e bambino con arcobaleno,
1998

Campagna Metauto Légèreté,
n.d.

Campagna Metauto Projet logo,
June 1998

Testa con frecce, 1998

Testa con rami, 1998

Uomo con frecce, 1998

Uomo freccia, 1998

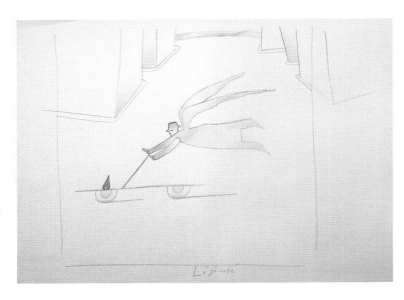
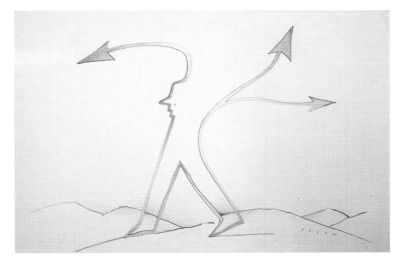

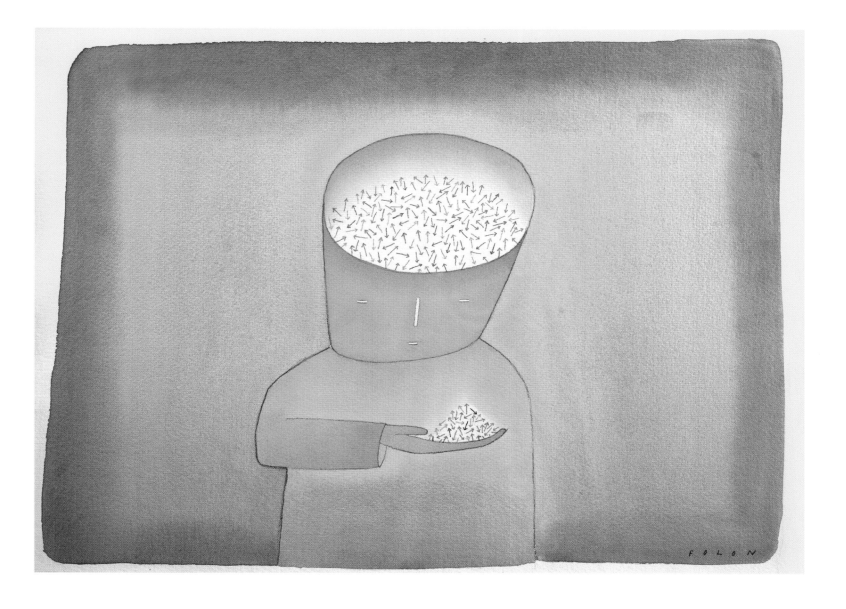

Tazza con nave, 1998

Senza titolo, Preparatory
Sketch, 1998

Senza titolo, Preparatory
Sketch, 1998

Un uccello in volo, April 1998

Senza titolo, Preparatory
Sketch, 1998

Senza titolo, Preparatory
Sketch, 1998

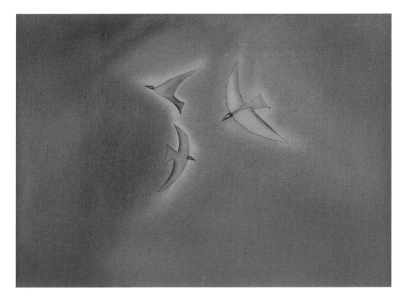

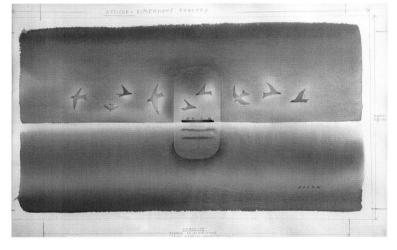

Uomo con uccello, 1998

Via Dante murales, 1998

Cielo e Terra (4 panels in single
frame), n.d.

Uomo che guarda il tramonto,
1998

*Le gaz naturel - Les couleurs
de la vie*, n.d.

*L'ami de chaque jour
(le gaz naturel) - L'amico
di ogni giorno*, n.d.

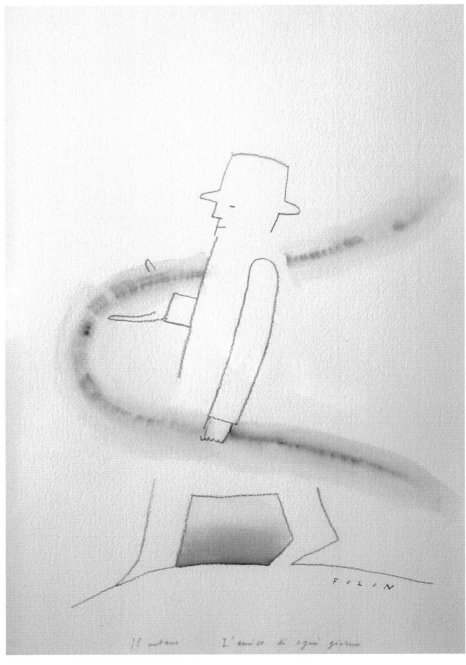

Le gaz naturel-Le mouvement de
la nature, n.d.

Une source de vie
(le gaz naturel), n.d.

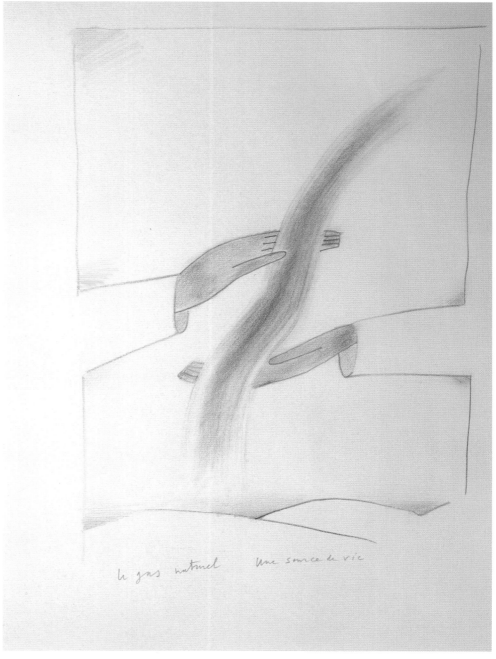

Proprietè, n.d.

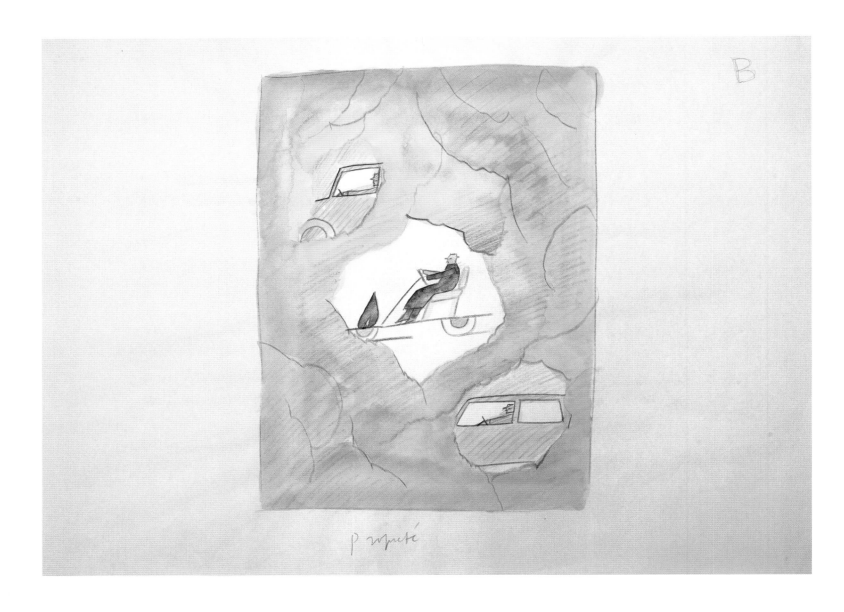

Nouveautè, n.d.

Proprietè, n.d.

Tranquillitè, n.d.

Ecologie, n.d.

Campagna Metauto Projet logo,
June 1998

Campagna Metauto Projet logo,
n.d.

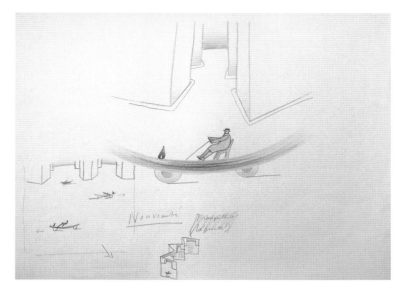

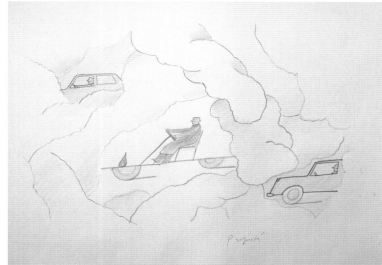

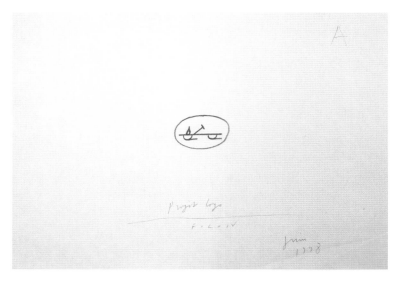

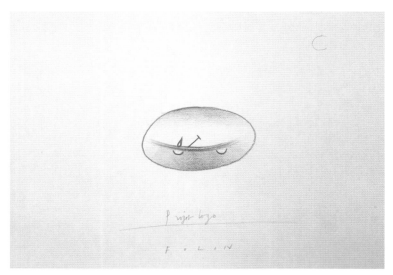

Senza titolo, Preparatory
Sketch, 1998

Proposta per logo ƐUROGAS, n.d.   *Senza titolo* Preparatory
Sketch, 1998

2000, n.d.

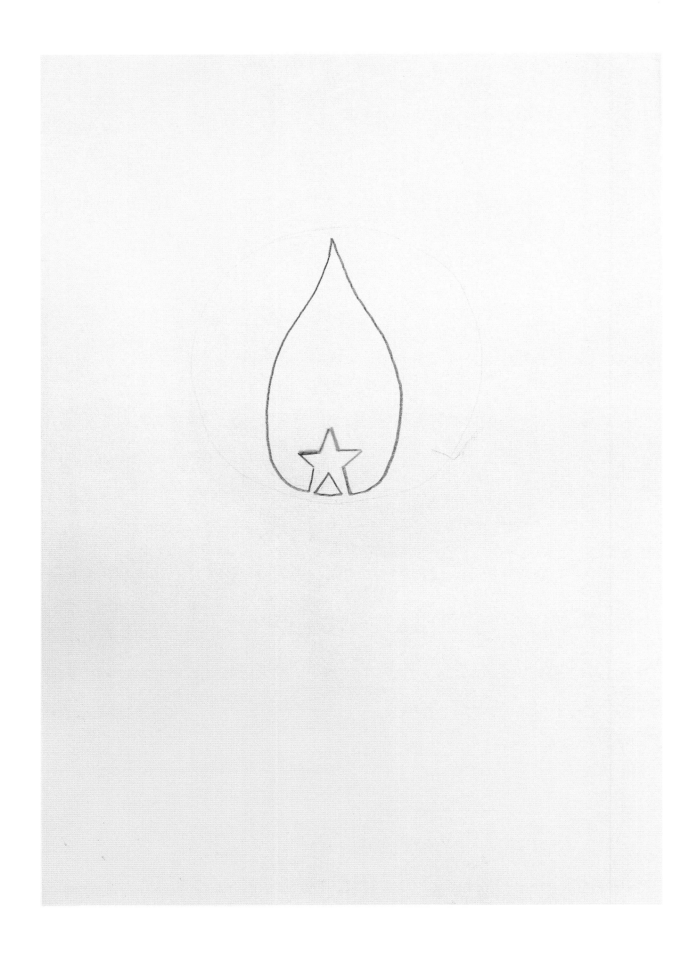

list of works

The list of works makes reference to the authors of the entire contents of **eni**'s art collections, including sculptures, objects and carpets not included in this catalogue.

PAINTINGS

Carla Accardi (1924–)
Bianco - nero - corda, 1989
acrylic on canvas, cm 89 × 106
[pp. 28–29]

Sergio Accorsi
Pozzi Marini, n.d.
oil on canvas board, cm 35 × 45
[p. 30]
Pozzi petroliferi, n.d.
oil on canvas, cm 50 × 70
[p. 31]

Valerio Adami (1935–)
Tavola e città, 1991
acrylic on canvas, cm 96 × 116
[pp. 32–33]

Ali al-Abani (1946–)
Raccolta dell'uva, n.d.
tempera
[p. 35]

Remo Aldini (1943–)
Mareggiata, n.d.
[p. 36 top]

Alipieri (20th)
Perforazioni petrolifere, 1962
oil on canvas, cm 56 × 88
[p. 36 bottom]

B. Andrès (1935–)
Mercato indigeno nella foresta, 1962
oil on canvas, cm 101 × 141
[p. 37]

Anonymous (early 17th c.)
Pergamena raffigurante San Filippo Neri entro riserva ovale a riccioli architettonici e decori floreali diffusi,
early 17th c.
parchment, cm 44 × 34

Stefano Arienti (1961–)
Senza titolo, n.d.
puzzle on color poster, cm 260 × 180
[pp. 38, 39]

A. Artiof
Astratto, n.d.
oil on canvas, cm 180 × 230
[p. 40]

Ugo Attardi (1923–2006)
Tramonto e fiori, n.d.
oil on canvas, cm 60 × 80
[p. 41]

Susana Attias (20th c.)
Los gitanillos gipsy boys, 1986
oil on canvas, cm 139 × 124
[p. 42]

Marcello Avenali (1912–1981)
Sogno di mille e una notte, n.d.
oil on canvas, cm 70 × 101
[p. 43]

Pierre Barat (1935–)
Paesaggio con lago, n.d.
[p. 44]

Paolo Baratta (1874–1940)
Autunno in tempo di guerra, 1919
oil on canvas, cm 161 × 135
[p. 45]

Francesco Barilli (1943–)
Esplosione di vita, 1980
oil pastel on paper, cm 100 × 150
[p. 46]

Sergio Barletta (1934–)
Accampamento, n.d.
oil on canvas, cm 100 × 200
[p. 47]

Rachid Benhadj (1949–)
Paesaggio con conchiglie, 1995
acrylic and mixed media
[p. 48]

Giuseppe Bertolini (1939–)
Senza titolo, n.d.
oil on canvas, cm 70 × 50
[p. 49]

Eraldo Bigarelli (1935–)
Omaggio all'Agip, 1988
oil on canvas, cm 70 × 100
[p. 50]
Paesaggio con alberi, 1990
oil on canvas, cm 50 × 70
[p. 51]

Gastone Biggi (1925–)
Variabile B.B., 1969
oil on canvas (*tamma bocour*),
cm 50 × 50
[p. 52]

Renato Birolli (1905–1959)
Figura di donna, 1947
oil on canvas, cm 65 × 48
[p. 53]

Alighiero Boetti (1940-1994)
Aeroplani, 1990
mixed media on paper with canvas backing, cm 65 × 135
[pp. 54–55]

Luigi Boille (1926–)
Al Raimy. Al Khayt, 1979
oil on canvas, cm 80 × 90
[p. 56]

Franz Borghese (1914–2005)
Personaggi, n.d.
scarf made of pure silk crêpe de Chine with hand-stitched hems, silkscreen design in 10 colors, cm 90 × 90
[p. 57]

Dino Boschi (1923–)
Motore città, 1970
oil on canvas, cm 55 × 45
[p. 59]

Cesare Breveglieri (1902–1948)
Chiesetta, n.d.
oil on canvas, cm 35 × 50
[p. 61]
Cortiletto, n.d.
oil on canvas, cm 29 × 42
[p. 60]

Antonio Bueno (1918–1984)
Figura in rosa, 1970
oil on masonite, cm 50 × 40
[p. 62]

Umberto Buscioni (1931–)
Un mare di cravatte, 1969
oil on canvas, cm 55 × 60
[p. 63 top]
Particolari, 1969
oil on canvas, cm 30 × 40
[p. 63 bottom]

Vincenzo Camerlingo (20th c.)
Carrozze nel viale, 1942
oil on canvas board, cm 37 × 52
[p. 64 top]
Mercato, 1942
oil on canvas board, cm 37 × 52
[p. 64 bottom]
Veduta di canale, 1942
oil on canvas board, cm 37 × 52
[p. 65 top]
Veduta di porto, 1942
oil on canvas board, cm 37 × 52
[p. 65 bottom]

Maurizio Cannavacciuolo (1954–)
Macchina anatomica: tartaruga napoletana, 1991
mixed media, cm 85 × 85
[p. 66]

Domenico Cantatore (1906–1998)
Natura morta, 1959
oil on canvas board, cm 50 × 70
[p. 67 top]
Natura morta di oggetti / Oggetti sul tavolo, 1960
oil on canvas board, cm 50 × 70
[p. 67 bottom]

Giovanni Cappelli (1923–1997)
Raffineria di notte, 1980
oil on canvas, cm 100 × 95
[p. 69]

Luigi Carboni (1957–)
Senza titolo, 1990
mixed media, cm 130 × 160
[p. 70 top]

Aldo Caron (1919–2006)
Evolvente n. 2, 1984
acrylic on canvas, cm 46 × 67
[p. 70 bottom]

Bruno Caruso (1927–)
Le Belve, 1965
oil on canvas, cm 98 × 98
[p. 71]

Michele Cascella (1892–1989)
Campo di carciofi, n.d.
oil on wood, cm 75 × 140.5
[p. 73]
Paesaggio invernale, n.d.
oil on plywood, cm 75 × 140.5
[p. 72]

Felice Casorati (1883–1963)
Ritratto di signora, n.d.
oil on plywood, cm 150 × 100
[pp. 74–75]

Umberto Casotti (1919–1991)
Astratto, 1965
tempera on cardboard, cm 70 × 50
[p. 77]

Bruno Cassinari (1912–1992)
Natura morta, 1968
oil on canvas, cm 98 × 130
[p. 78 top]
Madonna con Bambino, n.d.
oil on canvas, cm 200 × 250
[p. 78 bottom]
Ritratto antico, n.d.
oil on canvas, cm 160 × 80
[p. 79]

Enrico Castellani (1930–)
Superficie bianca, 1980
oil on shaped canvas, cm 100 × 150
[pp. 80–81]

Valerio Castello (1624–1659)
Ecce Homo, n.d.
oil on canvas, cm 120 × 95

Cavedon
Porto industriale, n.d.
oil on canvas, cm 60 × 120
[p. 82]

Bruno Ceccobelli (1952–)
Terra ascesa, 1992
mixed media, cm 100 × 80
[p. 83]

Giuseppe Cesetti (1902–1990)
Cavalli maremmani, n.d.
oil on canvas, cm 60 × 80
[p. 85]

Alfredo Chighine (1914–1974)
Natura morta con chitarra, 1949
oil on canvas, cm 80 × 65
[p. 86]
Paesaggio A1, 1952
oil on canvas, cm 81 × 90
[p. 87]

Hsiao Chin (1935–)
Figura astratta, n.d.
tempera on blotting paper, cm 35 × 29
[pp. 88, 89]

Ibrahim Kodra (1918–2006)
Il fiume verde, n.d.
oil on canvas, cm 50 × 60
[p. 153]

C.B. La Palombara (20th c.)
Omaggio a Guido Reni, 1984
oil on canvas, cm 80 × 95
[p. 154]

Guido La Regina (1909–1995)
Studio di reti a San Fruttuoso, n.d.
tempera on canvas, cm 100 × 70
[p. 155]

Lester (20th c.)
Seduti al bar, 1983
oil on canvas, cm 155 × 93
[p. 156]

Litz
Senza titolo, n.d.
oil on canvas, cm 78 × 125
[p. 157]

Silvio Loffredo (1920–)
Ballerina, 1968
oil on canvas, cm 100 × 70
[p. 158]

**Lombard School of the 17th century
(follower of Carlo Francesco Nuvolone)**
(17th c.)
Portrait of a Man, 17th c.
oil on canvas, cm 74 × 60

Mino Maccari (1898–1989)
Autovettura con cane, 1953
watercolor and India ink on paper,
cm 18 × 22
Supercortemaggiore, n.d.
watercolor and India ink on paper,
cm 18 × 22
Concimi-benzina-agipgas, n.d.
watercolor and India ink on paper,
cm 18 × 22

Mario Mafai (1902–1965)
*Natura morta con uova, pannocchie
e gallo*, 1929
oil on canvas, cm 62 × 49
[p. 159]

Egisto Magni (1952–)
Senza titolo, n.d.
[p. 160]
Senza titolo, n.d.
[p. 160]
Senza titolo, n.d.
[p. 160]
Senza titolo, n.d.
[p. 160]

Salvatore Mangione (1947–)
Senza titolo (palma e minareto), n.d.
oil on canvas, cm 80 × 70
[p. 161]

Francesco Manzini (1958–)
Interno Industriale con figura nuova,
1980
oil on canvas/acrylic, cm 161 × 121
[p. 162]

Giacomo Manzù (1908–1991)
Il falconiere, n.d.
pencil and wash on paper, cm 71 × 51

Federico Maragliano (1873–1952)
Sole e ombra, n.d.
oil on canvas, cm 80 × 105
[p. 163]

Luciano Maranzi (1932–2007)
Ritratto di donna, 1954
fresco on canvas, cm 71 × 52
[p. 164]

Angelo Marchetti (1930–2000)
Latina, n.d.
watercolor on paper, cm 53 × 34

Renzo Margonari (1937–)
L'ora viva, 1980
oil on canvas, cm 100 × 100
[p. 165]

(Barakat) Maroulla
Volti di donna, n.d.
acrylic
[p. 166]

Titina Maselli (1924–2005)
Greta Garbo, 1970
acrylic on canvas, cm 112 × 144
[p. 167]

Giuseppe Megna (1932–)
Minareti, 1980
acrylic on canvas, cm 80 × 120
[p. 168]
Ecos, n.d.
India ink and tempera on tracing paper,
cm 20 × 25

Franco Miele (1924–1983)
Campagna meridionale, 1952
oil on canvas, cm 50 × 80
[p. 169]

Milani
Senza titolo, n.d.
oil on canvas, cm 100 × 70
[p. 170]
Senza titolo, n.d.
oil on canvas, cm 100 × 70
[p. 170]

Sante Monachesi (1910–1991)
Piattaforma di perforazione, 1966
oil on canvas, cm 60 × 80
[p. 171]

Giorgio Morandi (1890–1964)
Natura morta, 1919
oil on canvas, cm 58.5 × 60
[pp. 172, 173]
Natura morta, 1941
oil on canvas, cm 29 × 44
[pp. 174–75]

Alliona Mossine (20th c.)
Il ciclo della vita, 1995
watercolor, cm 50 × 30
[p. 176]

Antonio Tono Mucchi (20th c.)
La villa, 1981
acrylic on canvas, cm 89 × 114
[p. 177 top]
Due luci nel crepuscolo, 1988
acrylic on canvas, cm 80 × 110
[p. 177 bottom]

Giulia Napoleone (1936–)
Rifrazioni, 1980
watercolor on paper, cm 95.5 × 131
[p. 178]

Vittorio Nattino (1890–1971)
Prato Fiorito, n.d.
oil on plywood, cm 58 × 84
[p. 179]

Neapolitan School (18th c.)
Squandering of Wealth, 18th c.
oil on canvas, cm 114 × 97
Departure of the Prodigal Son, 18th c.
oil on canvas, cm 114 × 97

Northern European School (17th c.)
Ester e Assuero, 17th c.
oil on canvas, cm 140 × 225

Luciana Notturni (20th c.)
*Colomba abbeverante (riproduzione
di un mosaico del Mausoleo di Galla
Placidia, V sec. d.C.)*, s.d.
mosaic, cm 22 × 25
[p. 181]
Piattaforma, n.d.
mosaic, cm 60 × 50
[p. 180]

R. Novelli
Fabbriche e case (cantiere), 1991
oil on canvas, cm 50 × 60
[p. 183]

Odim (20th c.)
Astratto rosso e bianco materico, 1963
oil on canvas, cm 50 × 41
[p. 184]

S. Kristen Ohen
Senza titolo, n.d.
acrylic on paper, cm 98 × 128
[p. 185]

Luigi Ontani (1943–)
Il giglio di Virgilio, 2006
watercolor on paper, diam. cm 98
[p. 187]

Giuseppe Pennasilico (1861–1940)
*Lavoratori all'Argano (bozzetto
del grande dipinto)*, 1920
oil on wood, cm 20 × 25
[p. 188]
Lavoratori all'Argano (cantiere navale),
1920
oil on wood, cm 200 × 252
[p. 189]

Roberto Perini (1952–)
Uomo sul letto tirato da due mani, 1999
watercolor on paper, cm 38 × 28
Gente che passeggia, 20th c.
watercolor on paper, cm 28 × 38
Il diario di un pazzo, 20th c.
watercolor on paper, cm 38 × 28
Il diario di un pazzo, 20th c.
watercolor on paper, cm 24.5 × 19
Il naso, 20th c.
watercolor on paper, cm 23.5 × 18.5
Nievsky prospeckt, 20th c.
watercolor on paper, cm 38 × 28
Il ritratto, 20th c.
watercolor on paper, cm 28 × 19
Testa sul libro, 20th c.
watercolor on paper, cm 38 × 28
Uomo che esce dal quadro, 20th c.
watercolor on paper, cm 28 × 38
Uomo senza naso, 20th c.
watercolor on paper, cm 29.5 × 26

Giovan Battista Piranesi (1720–1778)
*Plan of Rome and the Campo Marzio
and Caption*, 1774
1 panel
etching, cm 133 × 83

Alfonso Pone (1927–)
Paesaggio Dorato, 1958
oil on plywood, cm 79 × 99
[p. 190]

Umberto Postal (1949–)
Omologazioni, 1992/1993
fluorescent luminous panel,
cm 138 × 79 × 15
[p. 191]

Mario Pucciarelli (1928–)
Comparizione, 1966
acrylic on canvas, cm 80 × 70
[p. 193]

Enotrio Pugliese (1920–1989)
Casello ferroviario, circa 1960
oil on plywood, cm 50 × 70
[p. 195]
Porto, n.d.
pen and India ink and watercolor,
cm 19 × 27
La torre di Briatico, n.d.
oil on plywood, cm 32 × 100
[p. 194 top]
Torre Normanna, n.d.
oil on canvas, cm 50 × 70
[p. 194 bottom]

Domenico Purificato (1915–1984)
Testa di contadina, 1972
watercolor on paper, cm 76 × 58

G. Rab
Composizione, n.d.
oil on wood, cm 130 × 88
[p. 196]

S. Ricciardelli
Senza titolo, n.d.
oil on canvas, cm 40 × 50
[p. 197]

Fabio Rieti (1927–)
Le amiche, 1970
oil on canvas, cm 103 × 80
[p. 199]
Grattacieli, 1997
acrylic on canvas, cm 250 × 126
[p. 200]
Grattacieli e case dall'alto, 1997
acrylic on canvas, cm 250 × 112
[pp. 200–01]
*Ragazzo seduto affacciato alla finestra
sulla città*, 1997
acrylic on canvas, cm 250 × 122
[p. 201]

Virgilio Ripari (1843–1902)
Senza titolo, n.d.
oil on canvas, cm 120 × 80

Leonardo Roda (1868–1933)
L'aratura, n.d.
oil on canvas, cm 168 × 120

**Giovanni Francesco Romanelli
known as Viterbese** (1610–1662)
Roman Charity, n.d.
oil on canvas, cm 106 × 137

Roman School (late 17th c. –
early 18th c.)
*Figure Borne Shoulder-High
Accompanied by Putti Playing Music
and Drunken Bacchus*, late 17th c. –
early 18th c.
oil on canvas, cm 142 × 113
*Figure Borne Shoulder-High
Accompanied by Putti Playing Music
and Drunken Bacchus*, n.d.
oil on canvas, cm 142 × 113
Piazza del Quirinale, late 17th c. –
early 18th c.
oil on canvas, cm 96 × 130
Piazza Colonna, late 17th c. –
early 18th c.
oil on canvas, cm 96 × 130
Piazza Navona, late 17th c. –
early 18th c.
oil on canvas, cm 96 × 130
Trajan's Column, late 17th c. –
early 18th c.
oil on canvas, cm 96 × 130
Pantheon, late 17th c. – early 18th c.
oil on canvas, cm 96 × 130

Volpe
Senza titolo, n.d.
acrylic on canvas, cm 79 × 104
[p. 265]

Ellen Joyce Weinstein (1931–)
Uomo con bambino, 1985
oil on canvas, cm 114 × 94
[p. 266]

Mandy Wilkinson (1970–)
Senza titolo, n.d.
oil on canvas, cm 120 × 80
[p. 267]

Geira Auestad Woitier (1949–)
Fiori, n.d.
tempera, cm 50 × 30
[p. 268]

Yvan (20th c.)
Astratto, 1970
oil on canvas, cm 40 × 50
[p. 269]

Cesare Zampaloni
Roma-periferia, n.d.
oil on masonite, cm 53 × 73
[p. 270]

Emna Zghal (1970–)
L'eccellenza tecnologica, 1995
watercolor on drawing paper,
cm 35 × 29
[p. 271]

LITHOGRAPHS

John Absolon (1815–1895)
The field of Cressy, 1857
color print, cm 65 × 95

Gail Altshuler (1957–)
Gingham V, n.d.
color lithograph 6/10, cm 50 × 82
Gingham VI, n.d.
color lithograph 5/10, cm 50 × 80

Dominique Andrier
Woman Behind Door, n.d.
color lithograph 3/125, cm 40 × 30

Richard Ansdell (1815–1885)
The Waterloo Cup Coursing Meeting,
1840
color print, cm 72 × 120

T. Edward Barker
Sebastopoli, n.d.
print, cm 71 × 131

Mauro Benetti (1958–)
Fontana e alberi fioriti, n.d.
lithograph 51/100, cm 48.5 × 68.5

S. Bloom
Las brisas, n.d.
color lithograph 142/325 (painting
on glass), cm 120 × 93

Floriano Bodini (1933–2005)
Composizione astratta, 1991
lithograph 91/99, cm 50 × 70
Composizione astratta, 1991
lithograph 93/99, cm 50 × 70
Composizione astratta, 1991
lithograph 95/99, cm 50 × 70
Composizione astratta, 1991
lithograph 99/99, cm 50 × 70

André Bourrie (1936–)
Lointain Marin, n.d.
color lithograph 24/125

Domenico Cantatore (1906–1998)
Donna sdraiata in rosso, n.d.
lithograph 71/99, cm 50 × 65

Giuseppe Capogrossi (1900–1972)
Superficie 150, 1956
color lithograph 11/150, cm 43 × 60

Giovanni Cappelli (1923–1997)
Raffineria di notte, 1980
lithograph 36/125, cm 60 × 41
Raffineria di notte, n.d.
lithograph 100/125, cm 60 × 41

Carolio (20th c.)
La giornata, 1978
color lithograph 8/15, cm 178 × 135

Mirta Carroli (1949–)
Uomo seduto, 1974
lithograph and copper engraving 61/99,
cm 50 × 70

Michele Cascella (1892–1989)
Fiori, n.d.
lithograph AP
Fiori, n.d.
color lithograph CLXXXII/CC,
Prato Fiorito, n.d.
color lithograph AP
Prato Fiorito, n.d.
color lithograph XXXVII/LXXV,
Vaso di Cardi, n.d.
color silkscreen
Veduta di Portofino, n.d.
lithograph AP, cm 50 × 70
Vele a portofino, n.d.
color lithograph LXXXII/C

Cassol
Fiori secchi su sfondo scuro, n.d.
lithograph 48/125, cm 50 × 70

Enrico Castellani (1930–)
Superficie argentea, n.d.
silkscreen and copper engraving
42/150, cm 50 × 70

Giancarlo Cazzaniga (1930–)
Ginestre, n.d.
lithograph AP, cm 70 × 50
Ginestre, n.d.
lithograph AP, cm 70 × 50

Ceraio
Alberi, n.d.
lithograph 149/200, cm 70 × 50

Primo Conti (1900–1988)
Vaso con fiori, n.d.
lithograph 147/150, cm 50 × 70

P. Vincenzo Maria Coronelli (1650–1718)
Africa, n.d.
color print, cm 65 × 94
*Planisphere of the Old World (Africa
Europe Asia)*, 1718
color print, cm 50 × 64

Roberto Crippa (1921–1972)
Composizione Astratta, n.d.
color lithograph 38/100,
cm 42 × 52
Sole, n.d.
color lithograph 38/100,
cm 50 × 70
Sole, n.d.
color lithograph 38/100,
cm 47 × 39
Sole, n.d.
color lithograph 38/100,
cm 50 × 40

Giorgio Crocetti (1965–)
Fioritura Mediterranea, 2007
lithograph 51/99, cm 50 × 70
Prato con fiordalisi, 2007
lithograph 72/100, cm 70 × 50

De Brumia
Alberi in fiore con case, n.d.
lithograph (retouched with pastel)
106/150, cm 50 × 70

Giorgio de Chirico (1888–1978)
Tav. 4, n.d.
signed lithograph VIII/XV, cm 71 × 52
Tav. 6, n.d.
signed lithograph VIII/XV, cm 64 × 51

Luciano De Vita (1929–)
Astratto, n.d.
lithograph 95/99, cm 46 × 36
Astratto, n.d.
lithograph 97/99, cm 46 × 36
Astratto, n.d.
lithograph 93/99, cm 46 × 36
Astratto, n.d.
lithograph 91/99, cm 46 × 36

Hussein El Gebali (1934–)
Simphony of Calligraphy No. 14, n.d.
wood cut, cm 33 × 25

Mario Falchi (1950–)
Torre Eiffel, n.d.
lithograph 17/190, cm 70 × 50
Venezia, n.d.
lithograph 17/190, cm 70 × 50

Fernando Farulli (1923–1997)
Strutture e Ottana, n.d.
lithograph 97/99, cm 70 × 50

Salvatore Fiume (1915–1997)
3 Figure, 1 donna, 1 uomo, 1980
lithograph 100/100, cm 45 × 65

Jean-Michel Folon (1934–2005)
Cinquantenario, 1991
silkscreen 73/100, cm 50 × 74
Cinquantenario, 1991
silkscreen 25/100, cm 50 × 74
Cinquantenario, 1991
silkscreen 48/100, cm 50 × 74
Cinquantenario, 1991
silkscreen 52/100, cm 50 × 74
Cinquantenario, 1991
silkscreen 53/100, cm 50 × 74
Cinquantenario, 1991
silkscreen 57/100, cm 50 × 74
Cinquantenario, 1991
silkscreen 69/100, cm 50 × 74
Evasione (tonalità blu-rosso-giallo),
n.d.
color silkscreens 55/90-67/90-71/90-
81/90-82/90-83/90, cm 65.5 × 50
Evasione (tonalità blu-rosso-giallo),
n.d.
color silkscreen 72/90, cm 65.5 × 50
Evasione (tonalità blu-rosso-giallo),
n.d.
color silkscreen 86/90, cm 65.5 × 50
Evasione (tonalità rosso-verde-giallo),
1997
color silkscreen 90/90, cm 65.5 × 50
Evasione (tonalità blu-verde-rosso), n.d.
color silkscreen 48/90-50/90-51/90-
52/90-53/90-54/90, cm 65.5 × 50
Uomo che esce dal cielo (campagna),
n.d.
silkscreen 61/100, cm 49 × 74.5
Uomo che esce dal cielo (campagna),
n.d.
silkscreen 69/100, cm 49 × 74.5
Uomo che esce dal cielo (campagna),
n.d.
silkscreen 58/100, cm 49 × 74.5

Uomo che esce dal cielo (campagna),
n.d.
silkscreen 80/100, cm 49 × 74.5
Uomo con uccello, n.d.
silkscreen 79/100, cm 50 × 74
Uomo con uccello, n.d.
silkscreen 72/100, cm 50 × 74
Uomo con uccello, n.d.
silkscreen 70/100, cm 50 × 74

Gustavo Francalancia (1921–)
Architettura, n.d.
lithograph 50/125, cm 70 × 50
Architettura, n.d.
lithograph 109/125, cm 70 × 50

William Powell Frith (1819–1909)
Coming of Age in the Olden Time, n.d.
engraving-color print (engraver F. Holl),
cm 66 × 97
An English Merry Making Olden Time,
n.d.
engraving-color print (engraver F. Holl),
cm 61 × 92

Marcolino Gandini (1937–)
Intersecazione, n.d.
color lithograph 64/125,
cm 50 × 70
Intersecazione, n.d.
color lithograph 46/125,
cm 50 × 70

Giunio Gatti (20th c.)
Paesaggio, 1966
lithograph, cm 32 × 48

G. Gelia (1959–)
Casetta bianca e ginestre, n.d.
lithograph 17/150, cm 50 × 70
Casetta bianca e ginestre, n.d.
lithograph, cm 50 × 70
Casetta bianca e ginestre, n.d.
lithograph, cm 50 × 70

Gianbonus (18th c.)
Map of Persia, 18th c.
engraving and wash on paper,
cm 50 × 60
Map of Turcicum Imperium, 18th c.
engraving and wash on paper,
cm 50 × 60

Hoffman Godwin (1945–)
Artemis XXXIX, n.d.
color lithograph XXXIX,
cm 90 × 118

Peter Graham (1970–)
The flower, 1896
color print, cm 90 × 65

Piero Guccione (1935–)
Senza titolo, n.d.
color lithograph 11/20, cm 130 × 97
Senza titolo, 1988
lithograph 11/20, cm 130 × 97
Senza titolo, 1988
lithograph XI/20th, cm 96 × 130

Renato Guttuso (1911–1987)
Donna in piedi seminuda, n.d.
color lithograph on paper 48/80,
cm 69 × 85
Natura morta con cesto, n.d.
lithograph AP, cm 69 × 85

Shoichi Hasegawa (1929–)
Soir d'Orient, n.d.
color lithograph 94/110, cm 60 × 50

Hobart
Rolling in clover, n.d.
color lithograph 27/175, cm 135 × 107

John Hoyland (1934–)
First Man, 1993
color lithograph 29/90, cm 83 × 58
King Seal, 1993
color lithograph 38/90, cm 58 × 83
Thupelo Seal, 1993
color lithograph 35/90,
cm 100 × 75
Window to Nature, 1997
color lithograph 47/75, cm 40 × 50
Bertholdo W. Icheringe (18th c.)
Map of Groninga, 18th c.
print, cm 52 × 63
Illegible signature
Unknown II, n.d.
color lithograph 3/65, cm 45 × 60
Illegible signature
Unknown II, n.d.
color lithograph 21/75, cm 56 × 47
Illegible signature
Unknown IV - composizione astratta,
n.d.
lithograph 21/75, cm 56 × 47
Sebastiano Italia (1936–)
Albero con frutti rossi, 1987
lithograph AP, cm 60 × 70
Leonard Knyff (1650–1721) and **Jan Kip**
(1653–1722)
*Lambeth Palace, Seat of His Grace
the Archbishop of Canterbury*, n.d.
color print, cm 40 × 50
Ibrahim Kodra (1918–2006)
Palermo San Giovanni degli Eremiti, n.d.
lithograph 46/100, cm 50 × 70
Dino Lanaro (1909–1998)
Alberi Verdi, n.d.
lithograph 24/125, cm 50 × 55
Benjamin William Leader (1831–1923)
Conway Bay, 1892
color print, cm 57 × 84
Mino Maccari (1898–1989)
Venditrice di caldarroste, 1986
lithograph and wash, cm 70 × 50
Venditrice di caldarroste, 1986
lithograph and wash, cm 70 × 50
10/89, n.d.
color lithograph
10/89 Gli amanti, n.d.
color lithograph
10/89 L'adulterio, n.d.
color lithograph
10/89 Breloque, n.d.
color lithograph
10/89 Che tempi!, n.d.
10/89 La Gloria, n.d.
color lithograph
(the work has gone missing)
10/89 La Nuova Scuola, n.d.
color lithograph
10/89 Passo da parata, n.d.
color lithograph
10/89 Highlife, n.d.
color lithograph
10/89 Far West, n.d.
color lithograph
10/89 L'imperturbabile, n.d.
color lithograph
Proustiana, n.d.
color lithograph
(the work has gone missing)
Angelo Maggi (1958–)
Cane a 6 zampe, n.d.
lithograph 7/70, cm 35 × 50

Mann
Contadinella, n.d.
lithograph, cm 32 × 22
Francesco Manzini (1958–)
Esterno industriale con figura nuova,
1980
black and white lithograph 82/125,
cm 70 × 50
Esterno industriale con figura nuova,
1980
black and white lithograph, cm 70 × 50
Marenzi
Isola Tiberina, n.d.
series of 2 lithograph IX/XXX and
XII/XXX, cm 50 × 70
Umberto Mastroianni (1910–1998)
Astratto a sfondo rosso, n.d.
AP 2/12, cm 44 × 32
Cecilia Mayr (1955–)
Landscape, n.d.
monotype print, cm 146 × 90
Carlo Mazzoni
Parigi (à la grille), n.d.
lithograph 39/100, cm 50 × 70
Parigi (à la grille), n.d.
lithograph 19/100, cm 50 × 70
Parigi (à la grille), n.d.
lithograph 21/100, cm 50 × 70
Mercuri
Facciata di chiesa, n.d.
lithograph XIX/XXX, cm 70 × 50
Facciata di chiesa, n.d.
lithograph XVIII/X, cm 70 × 50
James Heath Millington (1799–1872)
Val d'Elsa, n.d.
color print 6/200, cm 40 × 50
Nama (20th c.)
Energy Series n. 5, 1975
lithograph 16/30, cm 69 × 89
Gabie Neville (1959–)
Akhar's Mausoleum, n.d.
lithograph 8/75, cm 82 × 64
Nicci
Astratto, n.d.
lithograph, cm 55 × 55
Astratto, n.d.
lithograph, cm 55 × 55
S. Ottavian
Castello, n.d.
lithograph XXX/XXX, cm 70 × 50
Pagano
Grande caramella, n.d.
lithograph and wash, cm 50 × 70
Antonio Pani
Paesello con prato, fiori e galline, n.d.
lithograph LXVIII/CL, cm 50 × 70
Dante Panni
Reportage 10/20, n.d.
color lithograph 10/20, cm 41 × 49
Pellizzotti (20th c.)
Bosco con piante e fiori, 1981
lithograph 67/125, cm 70 × 50
Evan Penny (1953–)
Jardin d'eté II, n.d.
color lithograph 281/385,
cm 70 × 53
William Charles Piguenit (1836–1914)
Beauteous Hampstead, n.d.
color print, cm 54 × 75
Prologo
Paesaggio, n.d.
lithograph 124/150, cm 36 × 50

Paesaggio, n.d.
lithograph, cm 36 × 50
Domenico Purificato (1915–1984)
Ritratto di donna, n.d.
lithograph 84/120, cm 70 × 50
Riptide
Canning, n.d.
color lithograph p.p., cm 30 × 35
Robinson
Rubina, n.d.
color lithograph 163/200, cm 38 × 38
Russo
Colosseo, n.d.
hand-colored lithograph, cm 50 × 70
Pietro Sanchini (1955–)
Riflesso A, 1966
color lithograph 10/25, cm 42 × 42
Emilio Scanavino (1922–1986)
Astratto, n.d.
lithograph 29/100, cm 50 × 50
Senza titolo (astratto), n.d.
lithograph 29/100, cm 70 × 90
Italo Scelza (1939–)
Dalla terra per la terra, 1974
lithograph 97/99, cm 50 × 70
Krugner Schuchart (engraver) (18th c.)
Map of Russia, second half of 18th c.
engraving, cm 71 × 36
Oranienbaum, n.d.
print, cm 36 × 71
Toti Scialoja (1914–1998)
Un colpo d'estate, 1980
color lithograph 79/125, cm 50 × 70
Un colpo d'estate, 1980
color lithograph 117/125, cm 50 × 70
Nelly Scott
Proserpine Romance, n.d.
lithograph 73/100, cm 83 × 105
Matthaus Seutter (1685–)
Deserta Aegipti, n.d.
color print, cm 55 × 60
Guido Strazza (1922–)
Miraggio, 1980
copper engraving 43/125, cm 26 × 20
Miraggio, 1980
copper engraving 15/125, cm 26 × 20
Miraggio, 1980
copper engraving 13/125, cm 26 × 20
Orfeo Tamburi (1910–1994)
Impasse, 1975
lithograph AP, cm 50 × 70
Case in campagna, n.d.
lithograph AP, cm 50 × 70
Piazza a Parigi, n.d.
hand-colored lithograph, cm 70 × 50
Piazzetta con panchine, n.d.
hand-colored lithograph, cm 50 × 70
Tetti di Parigi, n.d.
lithograph AP, etching and aquatint,
cm 70 × 50
Tetti di Parigi, n.d.
lithograph AP, cm 50 × 70
Nicholas Tindal (1687–1774)
A Map of Italy, 1750
color print
Angelo Titonel (1918–)
Manica a vento e cavallo, n.d.
lithograph 97/99, cm 70 × 50
Manica a vento e cavallo, n.d.
lithograph 61/99, cm 70 × 50
Antonio (De) Totero (1936–)
Fantasia Medio Orientale, n.d.
copper engraving 49/125, cm 27 × 36

Fantasia Medio Orientale, n.d.
copper engraving 97/125, cm 27 × 36
Davide Tranchina (1972–)
Senza titolo, 2006
lambda print on d-bond and Plexiglas,
cm 180 × 120
Senza titolo, 2006
lambda print on d-bond and Plexiglas,
cm 180 × 120
Senza titolo, 2006
lambda print on d-bond and Plexiglas,
cm 180 × 120
Senza titolo, 2006
lambda print on d-bond and Plexiglas,
cm 180 × 120
J.M. William Turner (1775–1851)
Dover, n.d.
color print, cm 52 × 66
Hastings, n.d.
color print, cm 66 × 51
Unknown
Prospetto della città di Edimburgo, n.d.
color print, cm 47 × 110
Renzo Vespignani (1924–2001)
Paesaggio industriale, 1974
lithograph 99/99, cm 50 × 70
Paesaggio industriale, 1974
lithograph 95/99, cm 50 × 70
Paesaggio industriale, 1974
lithograph 93/99, cm 50 × 70
Charles Whymper (Josiah Wood)
(1813–1903)
Shipe Shooting, n.d.
color print, 67 × 85
David Wilkie (1785–1841)
Rant Day, n.d.
color print, cm 61 × 73
The Reading of a Will, 1842
color print, cm 61 × 73

SCULPTURES

Anonymous sculptor (early 19th c.)
*Bust of youth viewed in profile on
circular base*, early 19th c.
marble, h cm 74
*Bust of Roman wearing a toga on
circular base*, early 19th c.
marble, h cm 81
Marble column on square white base,
early 19th c.
marble, h cm 126.5
Marble column on circular white base,
early 19th c.
marble, h cm 136
Marble sculpture of a youth,
early 19th c.
white marble, base 57
Pair of marble columns, early 19th c.
marble, h cm 115
Anonymous sculptor (17th c.)
*Vase carved from red veined marble
with false lid (probably architectural
decoration)*, 17th c.
marble, h cm 59
Anonymous sculptor (late 18th c.)
Christ, late 18th c.
boxwood mounted on wooden cross,
cm 132 × 65
Floriano Bodini (1933–2005)
Colombe in volo, 1997
Carrara marble, diam. cm 130

Volo di Colombe, 1997
bronze, cm 61 × 83.5
Volo di gabbiani, n.d.
bronze
Aldo Caron (1919–2006)
Statue of Saint Barbara, 1957
marble, cm 380 × 130 circa
Conquista di spazi, 1986
bronze, marble base
Antonio Catelani (1962–)
Senza titolo, 1992
white lacquered wood,
cm 190 × 115 × 15
Pericle Fazzini (1913–1987)
Il passaggio del Mareb, 1939
high relief
bronze, cm 300 × 295
Orrori della guerra, n.d.
high relief
nenfro stone, cm 300 × 210
Jean-Michel Folon (1934–2005)
L'Inconnu, 1993
bronze, cm 246 × 124
Noël-Jules Girard (1816–1886)
Sculpture of George Washington, n.d.
bronze, cm 62 × 32 × 22
Lombard school (16th c.)
Wooden sculpture of the Pietà,
16th c.
wood, cm 90 × 53 × 22
Francesco Messina (1900–1995)
Pugile, 1930
bronzo, h cm 160
Augusto Perez (1929–2000)
Scultura in bronzo-trittico, n.d.
bronze, h cm 170, lateral pieces
h cm 110
Giò Pomodoro (1930–2002)
Ritrovamento, n.d.
engraved copper plate, cm 3.97 × 123
Sante Rossi
Bimbi e Colombe, n.d.
wood, cm 109 × 30
Salvatore Scarpitta (1919–2007)
Face Trasp, 1991
wood, cm 46 × 72
Serena Tallarigo
Alternativa 2, n.d.
red marble, h cm 76
Giovanni Tessari
La sorgente, n.d.
Eugenio Tomiolo (1911–2003)
Statue for the Crèche, n.d.
wood, various dimensions
Unknown sculptor
Marble column, 18th c.
bronze base and capitals of the 19th c.
marble/bronze, h cm 250
Unknown sculptor
Model of buildings at San Donato
Milanese, n.d.
bronze, diam. 74 cm

RUGS

Bukara pendik (n.d.)
wool
Bukara pendik (n.d.)
wool, cm 272 × 177
Bukara pendik (n.d.)
wool, cm 205 × 345
Henigun-afshari (n.d.)
wool, cm 174 × 252
Heriz (1870)
wool, cm 358 × 300
Heriz serapi (n.d.)
Persian rug
wool, cm 500 × 400
Isphan (n.d.)
wool, cm 158 × 107
Kasak (n.d.)
Caucasian rug
hand-knotted rug, cm 180 × 115
Kasak borgialù (n.d.)
Caucasian rug
wool, cm 220 × 160
Keshan (n.d.)
extra fine wool and silk, cm 240 × 320
Keshan (n.d.)
cm 298 × 381
Keshan-bukara (n.d.)
wool, cm 302 × 183
Kirman (n.d.)
extra fine wool, cm 340 × 500
Kum (n.d.)
rug with Persian design (made in China)
cm 304 × 200
Kum (n.d.)
Persian rug
wool, cm 352 × 230
Kun (n.d.)
Persian rug
cm 400 × 295
Kurdistan (n.d.)
hand-woven wool, cm 205 × 290
Meshed-khoresan (n.d.)
wool and silk, cm 357 × 253
QAshqa'i (late 19th c.)
hand-knotted rug, 30 symmetrical
knots per sq dm, wool
Qum (n.d.)
hand-woven wool and silk
Qum (n.d.)
hand-woven wool and silk
Shirvan (n.d.)
wool, cm 192 × 120
Shirvan kila (n.d.)
wool, cm 236 × 156
Shirvan kila (n.d.)
Caucasian rug
wool, cm 300 × 126
Shirvan kila (n.d.)
Caucasian rug
cm 255 × 143
Tabriz-Serabend (n.d.)
Persian rug
cm 600 × 395
Tabriz-Serabend (n.d.)
extra crema, cm 315 × 400
Tabriz-Serabend (n.d.)
cm 298 × 381
Unknown origin (late 19th c.)
Shirvan Caucasian rug 105721
wool, cm 167 × 120

FURNITURE

Anonymous craftsman (18th c.)
Pair of terrestrial and celestial globes,
1792
h cm 53
Anonymous craftsman
Late Empire ormolu clock with case
in the form of a miniature temple,
circular dial decorated with putti,
standing figures at the sides and base
with scene in the classical style,
early 19th c.
bronze, cm 43 × 16 × 55.5
Barnard and Daniel (18th–19th c.)
Silver dish with centerpiece
dish (1856) / centerpiece (1770)
embossed silver, cm 32 × 47
Bayeux Factory (late 19th c.)
Pair of vases with painted scenes,
late 19th c.
porcelain, h cm 46, diam. cm 22
Chinese craftsman
Pair of modern vases, one decorated
with animals and the other with a
female figure and stag, early 20th c.
height with base cm 45
Elephant's tusks
2 elephant's tusks
ivory, h cm 195
Fossil, Middle Eocene
fossilized fish in calcareous olistolite,
cm 26 × 41
Le Roy et Fils (18th c.)
Pendulum clock, n.d.
clock decorated with lacquer and gold
Pietro Melandri (1885–1976)
Dish with decoration on red ground,
large majolica dish decorated in bas-
relief with mythological and imaginary
figures, 1950
oval majolica, cm 52 × 66
Amos Nattini (1892–1985)
Divina Commedia, 6 leather-bound
volumes, 1922
cm 84 × 67
Sèvres factory (late 19th c.)
Blue vase with flowers, late 19th c.
painted porcelain with bronze base,
2 bronze putti at the sides, h cm 45;
diam. cm 13.5
Joseph Schreiblmayr (18th c.)
Pendulum clock, 1770
clock with wooden case and bronzes,
h cm 51 × 32
Silicified Fossil Palm Tree, Quaternary
silicified fossil palm tree,
h cm 81, diam. cm 44
Silicified Fossil Palm Tree, n.d.
silicified fossil palm tree trunk, Libyan
Desert, h cm 181, diam. base cm 44
Silicified Palm Tree, n.d.
Silicified fossil palm tree trunk, Libyan
Desert, h cm 70, diam. cm 62
Unknown cabinetmaker
Louis XVI table with two small drawers,
late 18th c.
veneered with various types of wood
Garlands inlaid on the edge, vase inlaid
on the top

Unknown French furniture maker
(19th c.)
Pair of "guéridons," 19th c.
veneered with maple, ebony-stained
columns, h cm 65, diam. top cm 41
Unknown furniture maker (late 19th c.)
Table with two wings, two legs, four bow
feet and three drawers, late 19th c.
cherry wood, bronze feet
Unknown furniture maker
Sofa and two armchairs in Louis XV
style, 20th c.
carved and gilded wood
Xylon Palm - Silicified Palm Tree
(Pleistocene)
Silicified fossil palm tree, Jalo Jarabub,
Libyan Desert, h cm 156, circumference
base cm 73

Editorial project
and general coordination
Matilde Battistini

Editorial coordination
Virginia Ponciroli

Editing
Laura Guidetti

Graphic coordination
Anna Piccarreta

Design and cover
Sara De Michele

Layout
Elisa Seghezzi

Technical coordination
Andrea Panozzo

Quality control
Giancarlo Berti

Photograph credits
The publisher wishes to thank **eni**
historical archives for having kindly
furnished the images, all copyright-free,
collaborating in the realization
of this volume.

This volume was printed by Mondadori Electa S.p.A.,
at Elcograf S.p.A., via Mondadori 15, Verona, in 2015